FOR GIRLS 1993

STORIES

PAGE

FEATURES

STORIES TO READ

Printed and Published in Great Britain by D. C. THOMSON & CO., LTD.,
185 Fleet Street, London EC4A 2HS. © D. C. THOMSON & CO., LTD., 1992.
ISBN 0-85116-534-6

£3.95

HOME FOR CHRISTMAS

Remember Mum's golden rule, Wendy. Always put the key back safely, so it's there the next time it's needed.

You were a pup then, Sparky. Kevin was already mad about sailing — and our Gilly was forever trying new hairstyles. I can't wait to see her!

But, two days before Christmas —
Isn't it time we took down the decorations from the loft?
If you like, but I don't want to put them up until Gilly's here to help. She always loved that job!
Mum, it's Gilly on the phone.

Mum, I'm *REALLY* sorry, but I'm flying over to Paris in an hour! An important photo session's been arranged at short notice. I won't get back until New Year.

No Gilly either! It won't seem like Christmas!
Don't get depressed. We'll have a nice time, just the three of us — and don't forget Sparky!

So, a little later —
It's up to us to get some Christmas spirit going around here, Sparky. Tinsel, tree, lights, streamers . . . I think that's all the decorations.

Just then —
WENDY! WATCH OUT!
AH!

She's knocked herself out. Phone for an ambulance!

Later —
We don't think there's a skull fracture, but we need to keep her in for several days under observation.
Sorry, Mum and Dad. Now you really *WILL* be on your own for Christmas!

Don't worry about Mum. I'll book a table for dinner on Christmas Eve. That'll cheer her up a bit. You just get better soon!

On Christmas Eve, Reverend Samms came to the hospital with the carol singers —
God rest ye merry, gentlemen . . .
This is supposed to cheer up the patients left in hospital for Christmas, but it's not helping me forget I should be sitting round the tree at home, with Mum and Dad.

The doctor's decided you can go home after all, Wendy. Shall I phone your parents to come and collect you?
No need to bring her parents out. I'm leaving now and I pass right by Wendy's door.
So you can take me? *BRILLIANT!* It'll be a super surprise for Mum and Dad when I turn up! Good thing I've got my clothes here.

And so —
I can manage from here. Thanks for the lift, Reverend Samms.

The house is in darkness. Oh no! I've just remembered that Dad was taking Mum out to dinner to cheer her up.

I don't have my front door key, and now it's snowing! Some Christmas Eve THIS is turning out to be!

I wonder if, by some miracle, the old back door key is still hidden under the gnome.

Yes! It's here!
After all these years! But I don't suppose it will do me much good. These days, Mum always bolts the back door on the inside when she's not at home.

But, luckily —
SUCCESS! Now, what was it Gilly used to tell me? Remember Mum's golden rule. Always put the key back safely so it's there the next time it's needed . . . I'll do that straight away!

When the key was back in its hiding place —
That's odd. Sparky's not in his basket. Mum must have left the door open into the hall and he's wandering round the house.

I can hear someone in the sitting-room. We must have burglars. I'll slip out to our neighbours and phone the police.

Done it, Sparky! We've found the loose bulb.
KEVIN!

Thank goodness it's you!
Where IS everyone — and why aren't there any decorations? I come home to find the place in darkness and not a single streamer or bauble. I found them all on the landing.

I only managed to get in because I remembered the old key Mum used to hide under the gnome. I thanked my lucky stars Mum hadn't bolted the back door!
Me, too — but why aren't you headed for Canada?

The ship's had to go into dry dock. I wasn't sure I'd get leave so I didn't raise Mum's hopes. But, at the last minute, here I am!
I'll tell you what's been going on here while we finish putting up the decorations.

Meanwhile —
Thanks, Tom. That was a lovely meal.
Yes . . . I . . . quiet a minute. What's this on the radio?

The icy conditions caused a coach to leave the road at Devil's Bend.
That's near here!

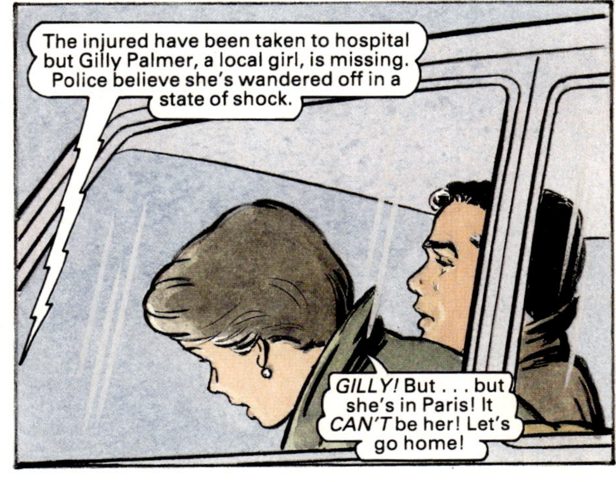
The injured have been taken to hospital but Gilly Palmer, a local girl, is missing. Police believe she's wandered off in a state of shock.
GILLY! But . . . but she's in Paris! It CAN'T be her! Let's go home!

And —
I — I think I'm dreaming.
HAPPY CHRISTMAS!

This is wonderful! I . . . I . . . can't believe it!
That just leaves Gilly to be accounted for. I'll phone the police.

Later —
Now that the police have confirmed it *IS* our Gilly who's missing, I . . . I . . . can't bear this waiting.
Let's raise our glasses to her safe return.

GILLY!

Oh, Gilly! Wh-what happened?

Much later —
I feel fine now. I must have got a knock on the head in the crash and wandered off, instinctively, towards home.

The next thing I remember is waking up here.
All's well that ends well. It's going to be a happy Christmas after all. Now please explain how it's come about that we're all together.

The shoot's been cancelled until the New Year. I didn't even stop to phone you, Mum, but headed for the first coach home. The rest you know.

What puzzles me is how they got in, even with the key. That back door's always kept bolted these days when we're out.

Before we left for the hotel, I drew back the bolts, just in case the children should come home. I suppose it seemed too silly to tell you about at the time — but I just hoped they might!

Hey, Sparky, come back with that key!

He wants to go outside. What's that dog up to now?

Good old Sparky! He's remembered Mum's golden rule. Always put the key back, so it's there when it's needed.
THE END

If Only

My hair is kind of mousey brown
My face is . . . well, it's spotty.
Mum says my figure will fill out
But now I think it's grotty.

In class, I'm sort of average,
No matter how I try.
I've never had a boyfriend yet—
To make things worse, I'm shy.

But, deep inside, I'm different,
There is another 'me'.
You'd be amazed how good I am
If you could only see.

For instance, snooty Pamela,
The beauty of the school,
Keeps lots of boyfriends on a string
And always plays it cool.

She doesn't know that, if I tried,
And used my brilliant mind
The boys would fall for me instead
And leave poor Pam behind!

I'd burst into the music scene
I'd sing and play guitar
They'll queue up for my autograph,
When I'm a top pop star!

I won't be just a pretty face
But witty, modest, kind—
I'd use my brilliant mega-brain
To win on Mastermind.

Mum wouldn't let me have a dog,
We haven't got a cat,
If only I could have my way,
I'd put a stop to that!

Out walking with my latest pets
I'd cause a stir indeed,
And everyone would flock to see
Two leopards on a lead!

Big Sue, the bully of our class
Had better mend her ways
'Cause I'd be a karate star
And put her in her place!

If only . . . there I go again!
The time's not right you see.
So, not a word to anyone
What's passed 'twixt you and me!

Remember, life is seldom quite
As bad as it may seem,
So, if you're sad, try this advice—
A girl can always dream!

JUNIOR NANNY

It rained that afternoon, so the children had to play indoors—
I'll share my soldiers with you and we'll have battles.
I — I'd rather paint a picture.
That won't suit Alan. He likes more active play.

But—
Alan's been sitting painting for the best part of an hour. Wonders will never cease, Anne. He does look as though he's keen to join in that game of soldiers, though.

But Alan stuck it out until tea-time—
Alan! That's greedy!
It's not for me, Nurse Chris! It's for my friend Jonathan. I'm looking after him.

One cake will be enough for Jonathan to be going on with. If he wants another, he can ask.
No he can't! He's shy. Jonathan, I'LL ask for you. I'm your friend!

Alan has certainly taken that little chat you had with him this morning to heart, Nurse!
That's for sure, Matron. Still, it's good that Jonathan has made a friend.

That evening—
I'm glad for Jonathan. Alan is very popular, so any friend of his will be accepted by the others.
Yes, and with Alan as his protector, I'm hopeful that Jonathan will find the courage to accept THEM.

A few days later—
Come and play with us, Alan!
Can't! Jonathan doesn't like playing football.
And Alan feels he must stay with Jonathan. Alan's missed out on a lot of fun these past few days.

One friend seems to be enough for Jonathan, Nurse, but it is very hard on Alan. He's taking his promise to look after Jonathan so seriously.
Yes, his friendship is putting a lot of weight on his shoulders.

That evening—
Matron says that Jonathan will be here at least three months. It's difficult to know what to do for the best, Anne. Alan likes to be active, Jonathan likes quiet games.
He's good at them, too. These little cardboard models he's made are really good.

If we helped him, maybe we could persuade Jonathan to make some more models and leave Alan to go out to play.
I don't think Alan WOULD want to leave his friend, unless . . . I wonder . . .

The next morning, Chris had a chat with Jonathan—
Oh, yes! I'd like to make a nice present for Alan!
But a present is nicer if it's a surprise, Jonathan. Alan mustn't see it until it's made.

A little later—
Jonathan is making a nice present for me, Nurse Chris, but he said I'm not to watch. Nurse Anne's with him, so will it be all right if I go out to play?
Yes, of course, Alan.

Later—
How's the present coming along, Jonathan?
We've a lot to do yet, Nurse Chris. It's going to be a super fort, for Alan's soldiers.

Some days later—
Nurse Anne helped me. Do you like it, Alan?
Yes! It's super, Jonathan! Thank you! I want the others to see my lovely present, Nurse Chris.
I'll call them, Alan.

The children were so impressed by the fort, that Jonathan forgot his shyness —
Can we play, too, Alan?
What do YOU think, Jonathan?
Yes! We'll all play together.

Well, your bright idea paid off, Chris.
Yes, it has. I'm sure that BOTH boys will be happy now.
THE END

PEPPER
the
PONY

Pepper! JUMP! You're nodding off again, you lazy good for nothing!
Who me?

That DOES it, Lucinda! I'll show you who's good for nothing!

So, that evening —
'Bye, old stable . . . 'bye, old cat.

Who was it who went to London to make a fortune? I know — Dick Whittington and his cat!

I'll have to go back for the cat! Turn again, Pepper!

And so —
Where IS that stupid cat?

Puss! Puss! We're going to London to make our fortune!

Two hours later —
Still no sign of Puss! I need a rest!

Next morning —
Pepper! STILL sleeping! You should take a lesson from Puss! HE'S up and washing already!

If only Lucinda knew! At least I'm good for SOMETHING, Puss. COMFY?

B

Wedding Belle

I envy you being a bridesmaid, Belle. I love romance and weddings.
Perhaps it will be your turn to get married soon, Liza.
I doubt it. I don't have much luck with boyfriends.
That's true, now I come to think about it. Liza's lived next door to us for a few months now, yet I've never seen her with a boyfriend.
Then —
It's Keith Laing from down the road.
Hi, Keith! Where are you off to?
A cricket match. I play for our local side.
Really? I like cricket! Do you need a scorer? Or someone to help with the teas, maybe? I'll gladly come along!
I'll do any job — cleaning, washing up, serving teas . . .
Er . . . no, it's okay. We've plenty of helpers, thank you. I must dash now. 'Bye!
Oh dear! It looks like Liza's her own worst enemy as far as young men are concerned. Graham obviously thought she was chasing after him and it frightened him away.
A few days later —
I've another wedding on Saturday. I'd better check my outfit. Oh! My shoes need a clean and the polish is finished. I'd better go down to the supermarket for some.

Liza works on the check-out here
I'm sure you can't manage all those boxes, Pete. Let me help! I'm not busy. Come on, let me take one.
No, no. I can manage, honestly. I'm only putting these here, then I've to collect up the trollies.

Let me help you with that job, then, I'm ace at steering dodgy trollies.
It's okay, Liza. I can manage on my own, thank you.
Oh dear! Pete couldn't get away fast enough. Poor Liza's TOO anxious to help.

The following Saturday —
Have a nice wedding, Belle!
Today should be a really romantic occasion, Mum. The bride, Valerie Dodd, runs a dating agency in town. Her whole life is concerned with making weddings happen and bringing couples together.

Later —
It's a super wedding, Valerie. And it'll be fabulous publicity for your agency, "Valerie's Valentines."
I'm glad you've enjoyed it. But, as to publicity for my agency, it doesn't need it now. It's closing down.

What! But why?
Because Jason, my husband, has been offered a good job up north. We'll be moving two hundred miles away when we return from our honeymoon.
I'll probably start another agency in my new home town. But I'll be too far away to continue running this one here. I had hoped to find someone to take it over from me, but I've had no luck.
I think I know just the person! Will you see her when you return from your honeymoon?
Of course.
No more chatting! It's time I asked my wife for a dance.
Liza would be good at running a dating agency, I'm sure! She loves romance and weddings!
A few weeks later —
Valerie gave me the job, Belle! I'm so looking forward to starting. At least this way there WILL be romance and love in my life — even if it's not happening to me personally.
A couple of weeks after that —
We finished school early today. I think I'll pop into "Valerie's Valentines" and see how Liza's getting on.
We wanted you to be the first to know! We've decided to get married! We're so grateful to you for introducing us.
That's wonderful news. I'm so pleased for you.
Did you hear that, Belle? I haven't been in charge of the agency for long, but already three couples I've introduced have hit it off.
That's great!

Before I forget, I must update the record cards of that couple who came to see me.
Okay. I'll leave you to it.
Oh — it looks like Liza has another visitor.

Is she busy? My name's Dan Jones. I work in the surveyor's office on the floor below. I've been trying to speak to Liza for days now, but she's always too busy to talk to me.
She is doing some work right now.

Well, I don't care! I'm not going to be put off any more. This time I'm *DETERMINED* to speak to her.

Liza! Listen to me. I want you to go with me.
What! I-I'm taken by surprise, Dan. But okay, yes. I *WILL* go out with you!

Brilliant! The old Liza would have chattered so much every time she saw Dan, that she'd have soon put him off. But the new Liza was so busy with her new job that she didn't have time to talk, and her apparent aloofness made him keen!

Coming to the dating agency hasn't just brought Liza career success, I reckon it might bring her personal happiness too. Who knows, one day I might be asked to be a bridesmaid for HER!
Valerie's Valentines
The End

Waiting for John

IT was the cream doughnuts that did it. Ever since I'd eaten two of them at my mate Jennifer's house the previous day, I'd been feeling queasy.

Jennifer's mum had bought a whole bag of the things. She said they were on offer at the baker's, and I can guess why! I reckon he was selling them off cheap because they were past their best.

I had felt dreadful all night, but hoped by the morning it would pass. To my despair, it hadn't. Now, at breakfast, I felt even worse.

"Some bacon?" Mum asked.

I clutched at my stomach. The smell of frying was nauseating.

"No! I couldn't!" I protested.

Dad looked at my untouched bowl of corn flakes.

"She hasn't even eaten her cereal," he muttered crossly. "Girls today don't appreciate good food! I hope she's not on one of those stupid, faddy diets."

"Of course she's not," Mum replied, then she smiled wistfully. "It's love! Today's the day John arrives!"

"Oh, Mum! Don't embarrass me!" I pleaded.

Dad rustled the paper, angrier than ever now.

"I don't know why you encourage her," he snapped at Mum. "She's far too young for that sort of thing."

But Mum ignored him.

"There's no need to be nervous yet," she told me firmly. "John's coach doesn't even arrive until twelve."

"It's *not* nerves that's putting me off my food!" I protested.

But Mum wasn't listening. She was too busy wittering on about how once, when she was a teenager, she hadn't eaten for hours before some re-union with Dad.

What with that and the sickly, fatty smell that kept wafting over from the frying pan, I couldn't stand any more. I got up from my chair and ran up to my room.

As I looked at John's photo on my dressing table, the memories came flooding back.

I'D been looking forward to John's arrival for weeks — ever since I'd first received the letter from him saying that he was spending part of the school holidays at his gran's and that we'd be able to meet.

I hadn't seen John for ages — for one year, six months and five days, to be exact. Before that, we'd seen each other every day.

We first met at Fulmere Infants, where I remember him as a stupid little boy who cried every time his

mother left him at the school gate.

At seven, we transferred to the Juniors together. John had toughened up a lot by then — become too tough, in fact. He and his mates spent every break and lunch hour running round the playground, terrorising the girls. The horrors!

At eleven, John and I moved on to Lakey Lane Comp. For the first six months I took no notice of the boys. Then some of my mates started going out on dates, and I began to look at boys in a different light. Oh, if only one of them would want to go out with *me!*

When John asked me out, I could hardly believe my luck. So thrilled was I to have a boyfriend at last, that I forgot I'd never actually liked John very much and I said yes immediately.

But it only took me a couple of dates to realise I'd made a big mistake. John was a right pain. We always had to do what *he* wanted, go where *he* liked to go. When we met *his* friends, we stopped to talk for ages. But if I saw one of *my* mates when we were out together, he'd rush me past before I even had a chance to say hello. I was fed up with it. The question was — what was I to do?

It was difficult enough getting a boyfriend in the first place. I still hadn't forgotten all those weeks of misery when my mates had guys but I didn't. But getting *rid* of a boyfriend . . . that, I realised now, was ten times harder!

How could I do it? I looked up the problem pages of my old magazines for some ideas. Telling him to his face seemed the most popular suggestion. But I couldn't do that — I just couldn't. I knew my mouth would dry up or my tongue would get twisted. The words would never come out.

Phoning was another alternative, but our phone's in the lounge. Either Mum or Dad might walk in when I was in the middle of chucking John. That, I decided, would be too embarrassing for words!

Not turning up for dates was the last suggestion. But what good was that? John and I were in the same class at school. If I didn't arrive for a date, I'd still have to face him at school the next day. Then I'd be back to square one — having to tell him to his face. I couldn't do it.

I got in such a state — wondering how on earth I was going to get rid of this boyfriend I couldn't stand. Then suddenly, miraculously, John solved the problem for me.

"We're moving away," he announced one evening. "Dad's got a new job — down south. I won't be able to see you again after this week."

Politely, I made out I was disappointed — but inside, I breathed a sigh of relief. Brilliant! I'd got rid of him at last!

So glad was I to see John go, that — when he pushed a note containing his new address into my hand and made me promise to write to him — I readily agreed. I didn't have to keep it up for very long, I decided. A few letters, then I wouldn't bother any more. Finishing that way would be much, much easier than doing it face to face.

The funny thing was, after a few letters, I didn't *want* to finish any more. John's letters were funny and interesting. I found myself looking forward to the arrival of the next one.

John himself seemed to change too. He wasn't selfish any more. He came over as kind and caring, and generous too. He often enclosed little presents for me — a pair of coloured ear-rings once, some hankies, and a make-up bag. He was really sweet! For the first time in my life, I decided I really liked him. He seemed to have become a genuinely nice person.

And now, at last, he was coming back. John had arranged to stay with his gran for two weeks. We'd be able to see each other every day he was here. I couldn't wait!

SUDDENLY I caught sight of my watch. It was half past eleven — time I was going to the coach station to meet him. I put my hand to my stomach and breathed slowly. I didn't seem to feel sick any more. Hopefully, it had passed.

But, halfway to the coach station, I discovered that was a vain hope. I passed a café where a big fat woman was sitting at a table in the front window. As I glanced in, she put a large cream doughnut to her mouth. It looked just like the ones I'd eaten the day before. The awful sick feeling swept over me again. I felt terrible!

It had begun to pass by the time I reached the coach station, then the smell of diesel fumes hit me and my stomach started churning again.

I was leaning against the wall for support when I saw John's coach pull in. He was here at last. Oh, why wouldn't this wretched feeling go?

Slowly the passengers disembarked. First, some old ladies, then a mother with two young children and a push-chair, a pensioner couple, and finally John. He came down the steps, a nervous smile on his face. I was about to run to him and fling myself into his arms — then it happened.

For hours I'd felt horribly sick, now I knew that I really was going to be. Instead of running to John, I turned round and dashed as quickly as I could to the Ladies.

A woman who was in there was really sympathetic, offering me tissues and asking me if I felt all right.

Funnily enough, I did. I felt fine now. Actually *being* sick seemed to have cured me at last. The feeling of nausea had quite gone.

Five minutes later, looking pale but feeling happy, I walked back out into the coach station. I expected John to be waiting anxiously for me. But he wasn't. He was nowhere to be seen.

Surprised, I started looking round for him. But he wasn't in the café, the shop, or the information office. Where was he?

Then, at last, I caught sight of him — sitting in the shelter near the bus stop for the bus that would take him to his gran's.

"Why didn't you wait?" I called, as I hurried over.

"Why didn't *you*?" he snapped angrily.

Then he pointed to his cheek.

"No need to ask that though, is there?" he continued furiously. "I *know* why you didn't wait — because of this."

I looked at him in surprise, at the cheek he was pointing at — and then I saw it. Going in a line from his ear to near his mouth was a scar. It was quite faint and really not that obvious.

I certainly hadn't seen it when he'd stepped off the coach. But he was terribly conscious of it. And, more than that, he thought it was why I'd taken one look at him and run away. What a mess!

I tried to explain about those wretched cream doughnuts and the way I'd been feeling, and how, finally, I'd actually been sick. But I could tell from his face that he thought I was making it all up as an excuse. How could I make him believe me?

Then suddenly the woman from the Ladies came along, and she saved the day for me. She bustled over to John, told him how ill I'd been and made him promise he'd take good care of me.

"Now do you believe me?" I smiled, when she finally walked away.

He grinned sheepishly.

"Yes, I'm sorry," he replied. "But I was so uptight about meeting you for the first time since my accident. I'm so self-conscious about it, I couldn't even mention it to you in my letters. I was so afraid you wouldn't like me any more."

I thought back to the wimpish boy at Infant School, the bully at Juniors, and the selfish creep I'd dated eighteen months before, and I smiled. What was a faint scar compared to personality?

"I can honestly say that I like you much, much more the way you are now," I said — and I meant it.

John's face broke into a grin and he flung his arms round me. I felt my stomach churn — but it wasn't a sick feeling any more. This time it was what Mum had said earlier, at breakfast.

It was love!

THE HONOURABLE S.J.

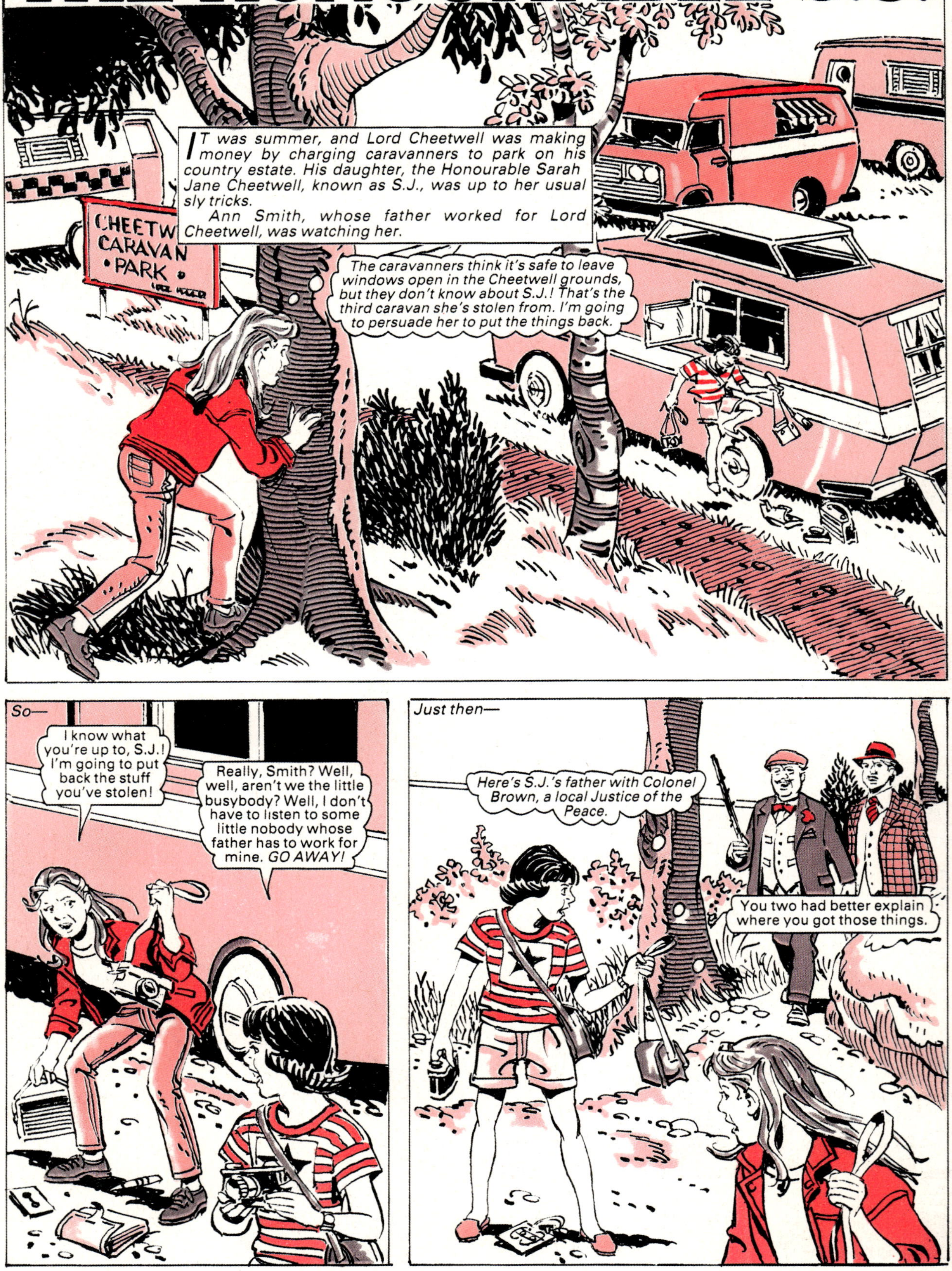

CHEETW
CARAVAN
PARK

IT was summer, and Lord Cheetwell was making money by charging caravanners to park on his country estate. His daughter, the Honourable Sarah Jane Cheetwell, known as S.J., was up to her usual sly tricks.

Ann Smith, whose father worked for Lord Cheetwell, was watching her.

The caravanners think it's safe to leave windows open in the Cheetwell grounds, but they don't know about S.J.! That's the third caravan she's stolen from. I'm going to persuade her to put the things back.

I'm sorry. I know now I shouldn't have had anything to do with taking things from the caravans, but Ann was full of the idea. I . . . I just got carried along!
She's blaming ME!
S.J., you KNOW I didn't steal!
Serves you right for interfering, Smith! Besides, I'll come out of this okay! A common kid like YOU might not, though.
A few minutes later—
You'll both do community service at a holiday centre. Quite informally — nobody needs to know you're being punished. You can choose between a centre for wealthy children and one for under-privileged children.
S.J.'ll choose to go with the rich kids. I'll get away from her by working with the poor kids.
But—
I'll work with the under-privileged children, Colonel Brown. I'm sure it will be very rewarding to help them.
WHAT? She's up to something!
I'm pleased with your choice, S.J. I have a special interest in that centre. What about you, Smith?
I'll do the same, Colonel Brown.
It's vital I keep an eye on S.J.
A few days later, the two girls arrived at Charford House—
I'm Mrs Benson, the organiser of this holiday centre. I feel honoured that we have Lord Cheetwell's daughter with us.
Pleased to be here, Mrs Benson. And this is Ann. She's the daughter of some fellow who works for my father. I thought it would do her good to come and help.

Minutes later—
We have a lot of support for the centre and so there's plenty of high-class equipment.
S.J.'s eyes are gleaming at the sight of all this stuff. I'll need to watch her.
And next—
This is our main function room. Ah, I see you've noticed the beautiful silver rose bowl. It belongs to the Charford family. Tradition has it that it's always kept here.
Soon—
Right! This bed near the window's mine, and I'll have the wardrobe. You can keep your clothes in your suitcase. Oh, roll on teatime. I'm starving!
S.J.'s so selfish. I'm hungry, too, though. We'll go down to the dining room in a few minutes.
Shortly—
S.J. and I could serve tea, Mrs Benson. It would give us a chance to get to know the children.
Excellent. This was YOUR idea, I suppose, Sarah Jane. I've told the children all about you.
Trust S.J. not to correct Mrs Benson. Still, she's furious at having to serve!
But—
Are you VERY rich?
Do you really live in a great big house?
Typical! S.J. loves attention. She'll use these children!
Sure enough, later—
We're supposed to be supervising, but S.J.'s got the children watching HER, while SHE shows off!

And—
See? Hit the ball at the highest point.
I don't care whether the brats understand or not! This is a good chance for me to practise my service!
One day—
S.J., we're to take the children to town this afternoon. They're being given some spending money. I think having money will be a new experience for most of them.
Ugh! Those guttersnipes have too much expensive equipment and now they're to have money as well? It's disgraceful!
But, later—
I'm looking forward to taking the children to town, Mrs Benson. It's a lovely idea.
S.J.'s so false! She'll find a way to turn the situation to her advantage.
So, that afternoon—
It's S.J.'s birthday tomorrow.
I happen to know S.J.'s birthday is NEXT month. She wants these poor kids to spend their money on her! How awful!
Later, in town—
EVERY ITEM A REAL BARGAIN!
What about this?
I think S.J. would like this.
S.J.'s gone off on her own, and the children want to buy these awful cheap trinkets. I hate to think of them spending on something S.J. will just throw in the bin.
You know, S.J. loves fudge, caramels and Turkish delight. What about buying some of that?
Yes.
SALE
Great.

The next afternoon—
The children have been very generous spending their money like this. They must admire S.J. very much.
What they couldn't know, Mrs Benson, is that S.J. is equally generous. I know she'll let the children have these treats!
So—
S.J.'s furious, but she has to pretend to be pleased at sharing her sweets. Serves her right!
A few days later—
Do you like our decorations? We made them ourselves.
The children are so excited preparing for the disco. S.J.'s doing as little as possible, as usual. She's fooling around with the tape deck. Ooh! That music's really loud.
Later—
So you've got the directions to the function room? It's ready for the disco. The only thing is, you'll be about twenty hours early. Ha! Ha! See you later then, Rodney.
Rodney! S.J.'s cousin! He's a shady character. They're up to no good. Right, S.J., I'm going to catch you out, whatever you're up to.
That night—
There she goes. I'll follow.

A few moments later—
So THAT'S it! They're stealing the silver rose bowl! Right, I'll switch on the outside floodlights. That should stop them!
THE LIGHTS! I'm off, S.J.
Somebody must have heard us! I'll say I surprised a thief stealing the rose bowl, and I saved it! Yes — that'll look good!
But—
Hello, S.J. Your little plot's failed. Now, I suggest you put the rose bowl back, before I fetch Mrs Benson.
YOU! YOU switched on the light? Ha! Don't be a fool, Smith! The likes of you can't threaten ME!
Switch those lights off immediately, Smith, before somebody notices! Otherwise I'll say I've just stopped you from stealing this bowl! I've framed you before! That's why we're here, pretending to be interested in these dreadful brats and that stupid old crow, Mrs Benson.
You'll never get one up on me, and why should you? You're no better than the brats here!
The next evening was the disco—
S.J.'s as surprised as I am to see Colonel Brown arrive, but she's sucking up to him!

S.J.'s been excellent, Colonel Brown. I can't say the same of Ann, I'm afraid. She's a very different character.
You BET we are, Mrs Benson!

The disco's ready to begin, Colonel Brown. Would you have the first dance with me?
Typical attention – seeking behaviour!

But, when the tape was switched on—
. . . THAT'S WHY WE'RE HERE, PRETENDING TO BE INTERESTED IN THESE DREADFUL BRATS AND THAT STUPID OLD CROW, MRS BENSON.
Now S.J. will get all the attention she wants!

Within the hour, the truth was out and S.J. was sent away—
For once, S.J. hadn't got a thing to say for herself. The tape said it all!

Ann, I misjudged you. You aren't a thief. There's no need for you to spend your summer here, after all.
But I'd love to stay, Colonel Brown. In fact, I'll go back in and help with the disco.

A few minutes later—
Here's the music tape that SHOULD have been played to start the disco. I'll put it back. Swapping it for the one I recorded in here last night when I faced up to S.J. was very successful — S.J.'s gone. Here's to a good summer!
THE END

"YOU'RE JUST JEALOUS!"
AMY CARTER and Lucy Binns were best friends and always went everywhere together. One day, during the school holidays . . .
ATCHOO! ATCHOO! Oh dear! I don't feel too good. I think I'd better stay in bed tomorrow.
Bad luck, Amy. We'd planned to go to the cinema, too. Never mind. We'll go when you're better.
Next morning —
Amy's mum says she'll probably have to stay in bed for several days. Life's going to be really dull without her.
Just then —
Excuse me. Is this house called "Greenways"?
That's right. Are you our new paper boy?
Only a temporary one while yours is on holiday. I'm finding it really hard because a lot of houses round here have names and no numbers.
I'll help you if you like.
It'll give me something to do.

Soon —
That's the last one. You've been a great help, Lucy. How about I buy you a cola in return?
Thanks!
Chris is really nice. I thought today would be a drag without Amy, but I'm enjoying chatting to him.

I've enjoyed being with you. How about coming out with me tomorrow evening, Lucy?
TELEPHONE
That'd be great! And I'll help you again with the papers in the morning if you like.

That evening —
My first-ever proper date! Just wait till I tell Amy.
Hi! I thought we'd go to the local cinema. There's a great film on.
That's the film I promised I'd go to with Amy. Never mind, I can see it twice. I shan't let her down. She's too important to me!

Next day —
Hi — it's me! I'm better at last.
Great to see you, Amy! Do I have some news for YOU!

. . . so Chris asked me if I'd go steady. He's ace! I'm to see him on Thursday and Saturday nights.
A boyfriend! I won't see much of Lucy if she's dating someone. Still, I mustn't complain. It was bound to happen eventually.
But not Friday? Great. We can go to the cinema then.

Yes. The film's really good.
You've SEEN it?

Later —

BOOKS and CARDS

Oh! There he is. And he's with another girl. Just wait till I tell Lucy!

And so —

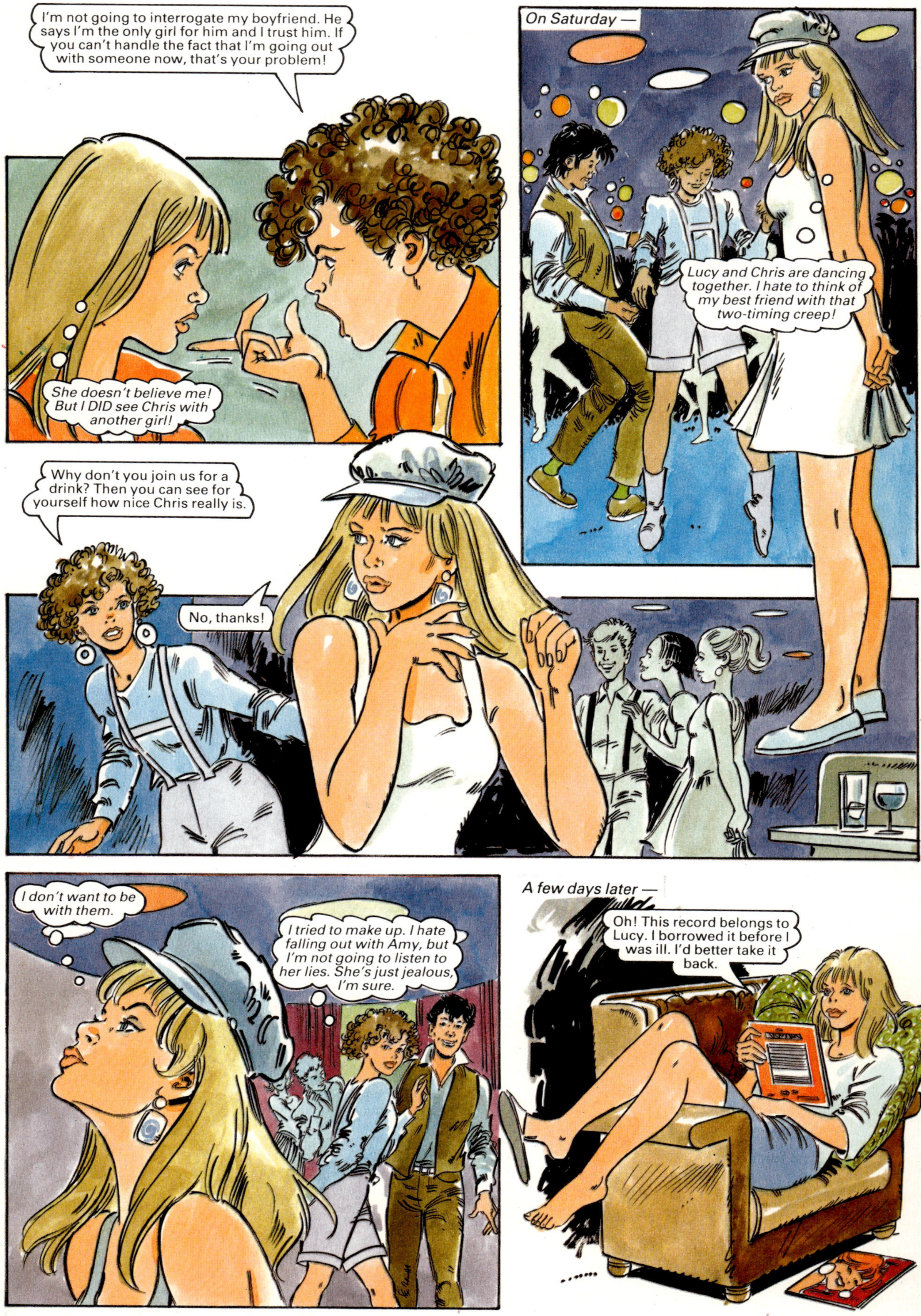

I'm not going to interrogate my boyfriend. He says I'm the only girl for him and I trust him. If you can't handle the fact that I'm going out with someone now, that's your problem!

She doesn't believe me! But I DID see Chris with another girl!

On Saturday —

Lucy and Chris are dancing together. I hate to think of my best friend with that two-timing creep!

Why don't you join us for a drink? Then you can see for yourself how nice Chris really is.

No, thanks!

And so —
Here's your record, Lucy.
Thanks, Amy.
SUNDAY

HI! Here's your dad's paper.
Hello, Chris!
Blow! He WOULD turn up.

This is Amy. She's . . . um . . . a friend of mine.
Huh! I'm not sure if I am any more. Not since Chris came on the scene, and I saw him with that girl.

HEY! There IS the girl. This is my chance to prove to Lucy that I WAS right all along.
Isn't that a friend of yours, Chris? A very CLOSE friend?

WHERE? Oh, that's my sister, Laura. Over here, sis!
His SISTER? Oh, NO!

Meet my girlfriend, Laura.
Hi! I've heard a lot about you, Lucy.
I'll leave. They don't want me around. I've been a fool, jumping to the wrong conclusions — and I've lost my best friend.

But, that evening —
Visitor for you, Amy.
Hi! Chris is outside — with a friend, Nick. We were wondering if you'd come out with us.
Y-you mean you forgive me, Lucy?

Of course I do! I realised from your face that it must have been Laura you saw Chris with. We've been best friends for too long to let a thing like that come between us. Come and meet the boys.

And, at the end of the evening —
Well! What do you think? Do you like Chris now?
Yes. He's really nice.

But I like his friend Nick even better!
DISCO BAR
THE END

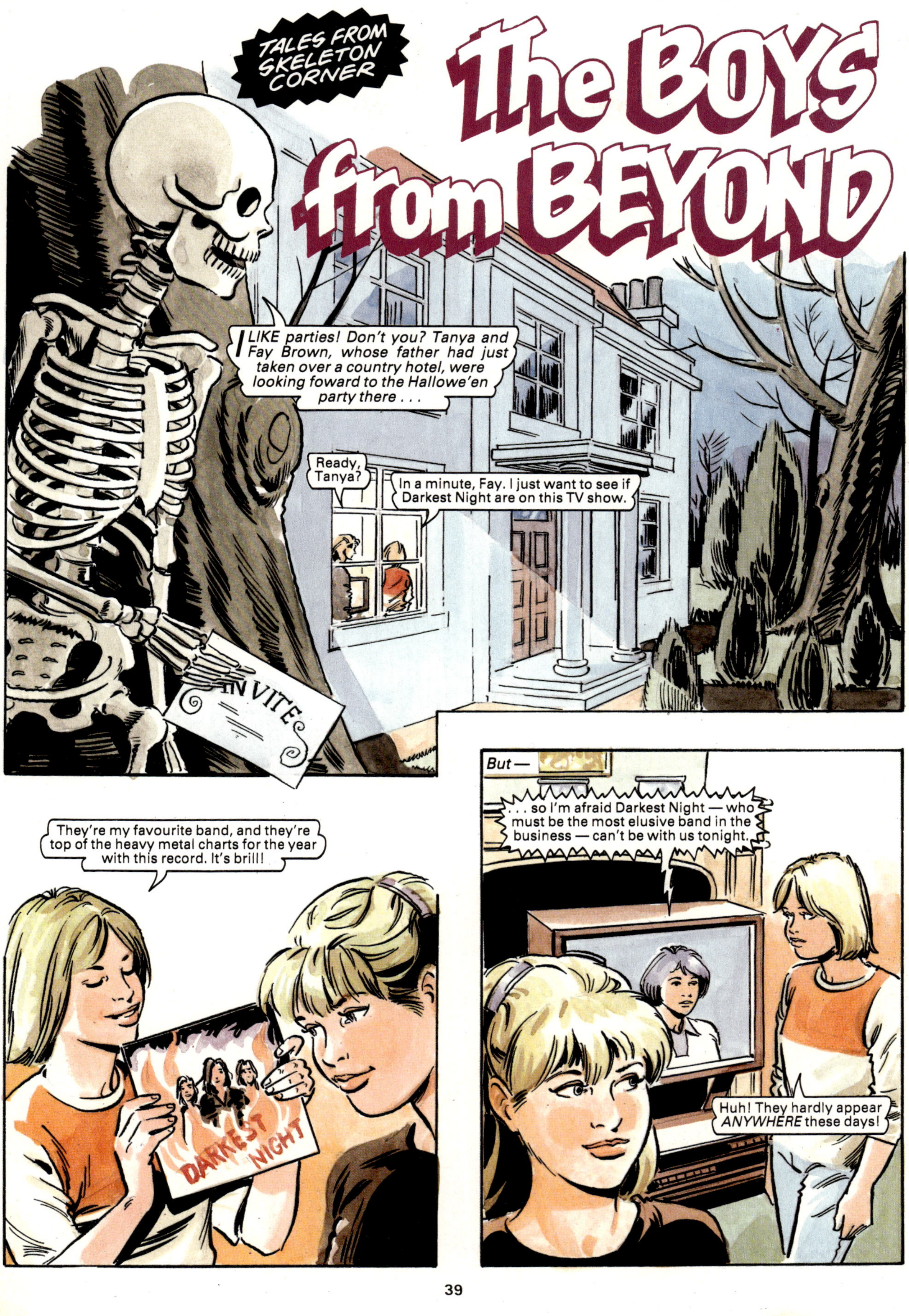

TALES FROM SKELETON CORNER

The BOYS from BEYOND

I LIKE parties! Don't you? Tanya and Fay Brown, whose father had just taken over a country hotel, were looking foward to the Hallowe'en party there . . .

INVITE

Ready, Tanya?

In a minute, Fay. I just want to see if Darkest Night are on this TV show.

Never mind. Dad's booked a band for this party tonight. Let's go and see what *THEY'RE* like . . .

HALLOWEEN PARTY
FANCY DRESS OPTIONAL
Mmmm, they don't really look my type!
Nor mine! In fact, I think this party's going to be a waste of time for us.

The guests are all about the same age as Mum and Dad — or older!
I'M not!

I'm Luke, from the village. I came here with my parents but — apart from meeting you two — I agree it looks like being a boring night.
WHOO-OOOH!

Grown-ups are worse than little kids, sometimes!
I wish it were a *REAL* ghost. That would liven things up a bit!

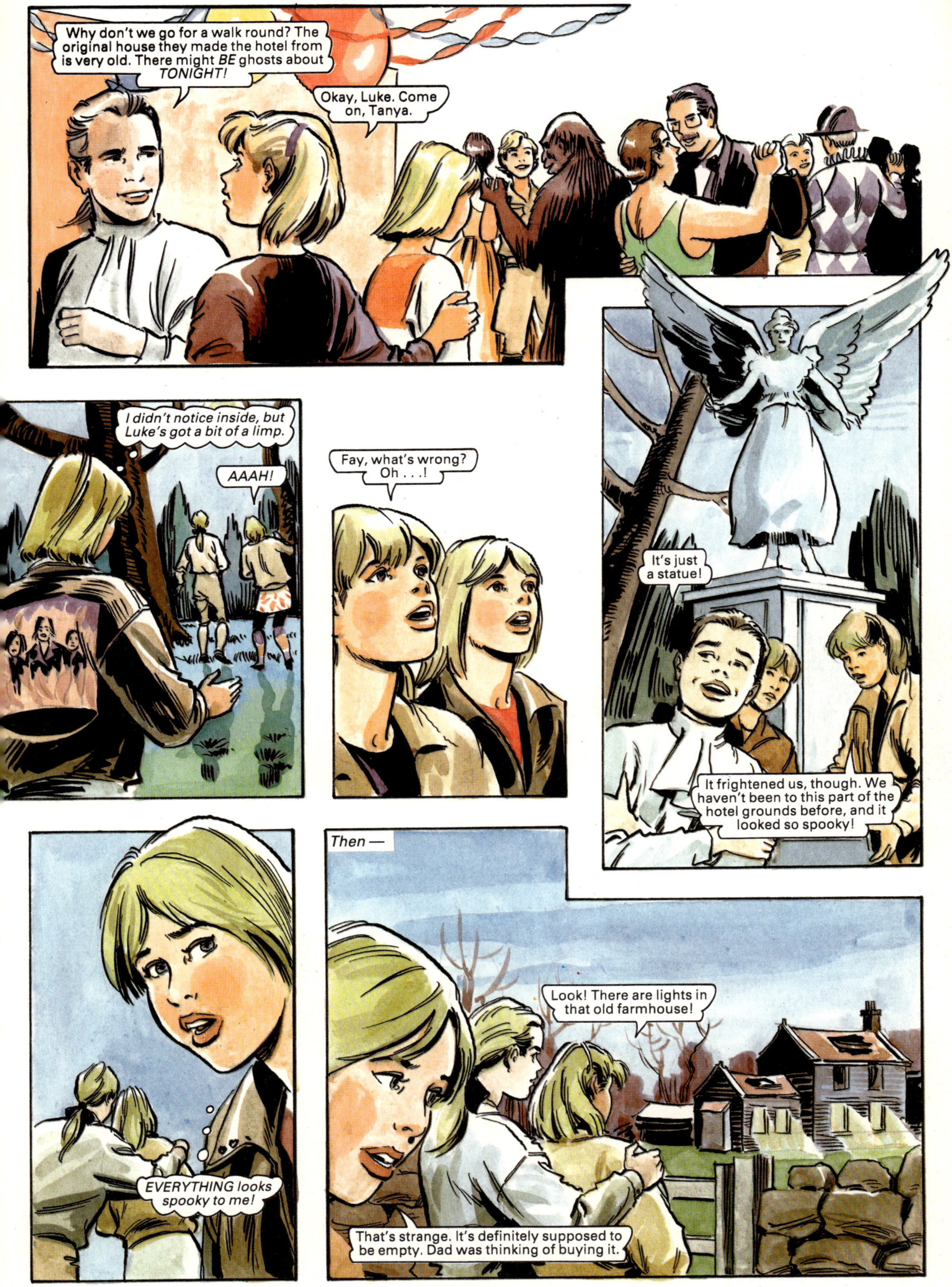

Why don't we go for a walk round? The original house they made the hotel from is very old. There might *BE* ghosts about *TONIGHT!*
Okay, Luke. Come on, Tanya.

It's just a statue!
It frightened us, though. We haven't been to this part of the hotel grounds before, and it looked so spooky!

We'll have a peep and find out what's going on.
I don't . . .
We'll be all right with Luke . . . He isn't scared . . .

I . . . don't believe it!
It's Darkest Night. We must go in and meet them!

You're my favourite band! I've got all your records — and everything.

But . . . what are you doing *HERE?*
Just practising some songs for our new album.

Oh, no!

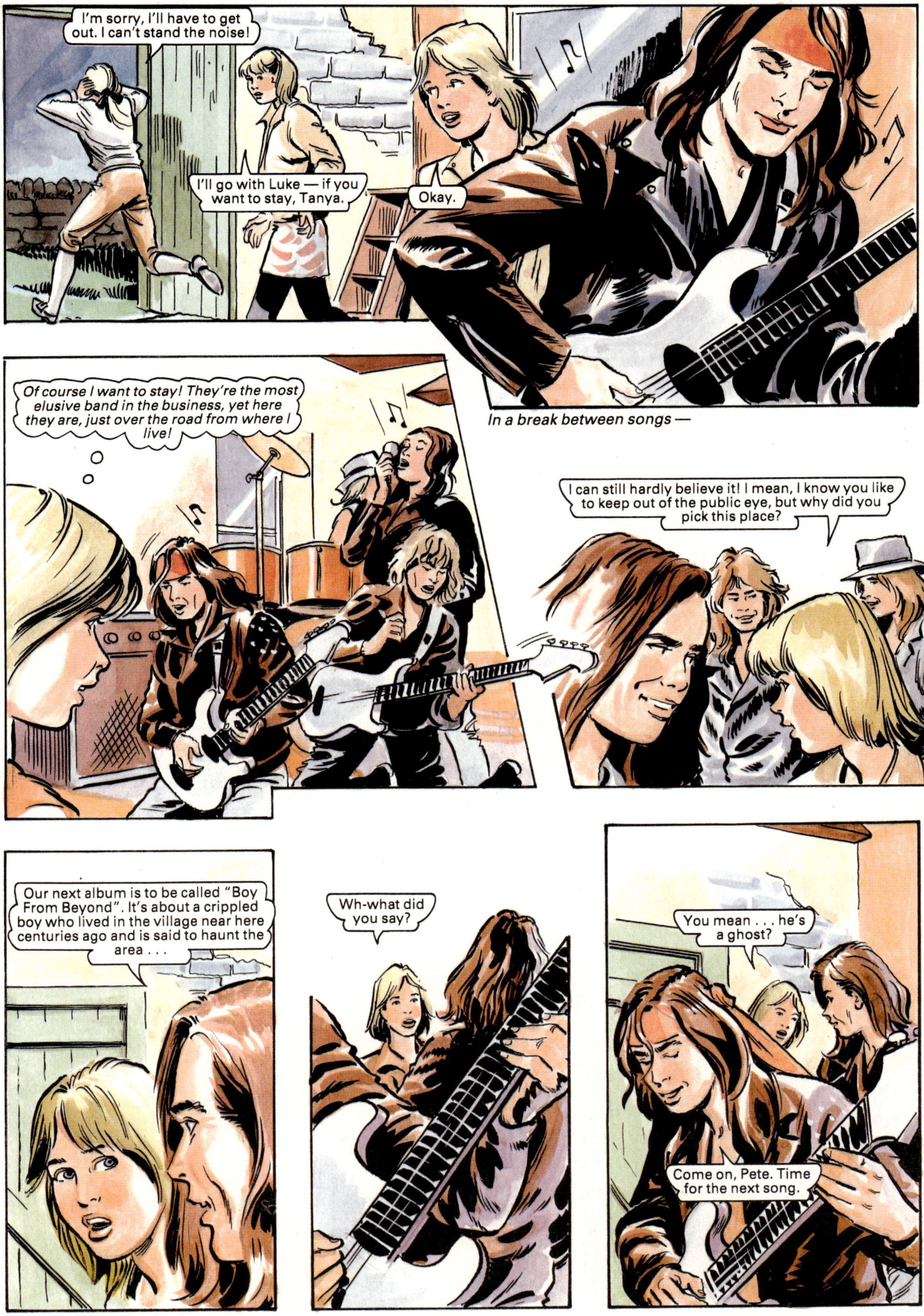

I'm sorry, I'll have to get out. I can't stand the noise!

I'll go with Luke — if you want to stay, Tanya.

Okay.

Of course I want to stay! They're the most elusive band in the business, yet here they are, just over the road from where I live!

In a break between songs —

I can still hardly believe it! I mean, I know you like to keep out of the public eye, but why did you pick this place?

A crippled boy? Luke has a slight limp . . . and we know NOTHING about him . . .
He said he came from the village, but I've never seen him there!
And the way he didn't jump at the statue . . . Maybe he's used to that sort of thing . . . in a quiet graveyard or somewhere!
Certainly he doesn't like noise . . . and I bet those clothes AREN'T fancy dress at all. They're the real thing, that he's worn for hundreds of years!
Luke's the "boy from beyond"! and he's out there — WITH FAY!
That boy who was in here with my sister is the one you're singing about! He's a ghost and he's taken her outside —
Don't worry . . .

. . . he won't hurt your sister, even if he *IS* a ghost, Tanya. Ghosts visit, then have to go again . . .

They just suddenly vanish!

WHAT'S THAT?

. . . suddenly vanish, Tanya . . .

Fay! Are you all right? I was so worried!

But, inside —
WHAT? HOW . . .?
There was no heat in the flames as the band vanished —
Where has the band gone? I know they're famous for being elusive, but they've got away fast!
Yeh, they . . .
You look as though you've seen a ghost!
No . . .
They just suddenly vanished. As the singer said — ALL ghosts do! THEY were the boys from beyond!
THE END

EASTER PARADE

Hallmark gives your Easter eggs the glamour treatment!

Materials: (for each figure)
A sheet of HALLMARK gift-wrap paper
4 strips of thin white paper, each 10 x 30 cm.
Thin white card
Stiff card (cereal carton, etc)
A large (size 1) light brown egg, hard-boiled
Knitting yarn for hair (double-knit or 4-ply)
Felt pen/s
Clear adhesive
Glue stick (optional)
Adhesive tape (optional)

1. Roll up one strip of white paper to form a tube for the egg to rest on, then tape or stick the join. Roll the remaining strips up and allow them to open out inside the tube.
2. Wrap a 10 x 15 cm piece of **HALLMARK** paper round the tube and tape the overlap. (For a satisfactory result, it is important to use good quality gift-wrap).

FIGURE 1: CAPE

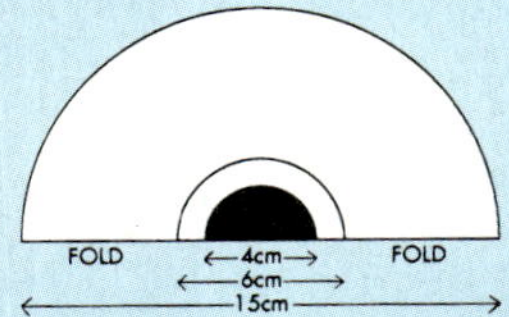

FIGURE 2: CAPE

SNIP

3. To make the cape, fold a piece of gift-wrap in half and draw semi-circles as figure 1. Cut round the outer edge (with pinking shears, if possible), and cut away the shaded area in the centre.
4. Stick the paper together around the inner and outer cut edges.
5. Snip the inner edge to the marked line so that it forms tiny tabs (figure 2).
6. Bend the tabs DOWN, then run a line of glue round the top of the tube on the INSIDE, and press the tabs against it. Stick the two front edges of the cape vertically to the tube, as illustrated.
7. Following the measurements in figure 3, prepare another piece of paper in the same way (steps 3, 4 and 5), for the skirt.

FIGURE 3: SKIRT

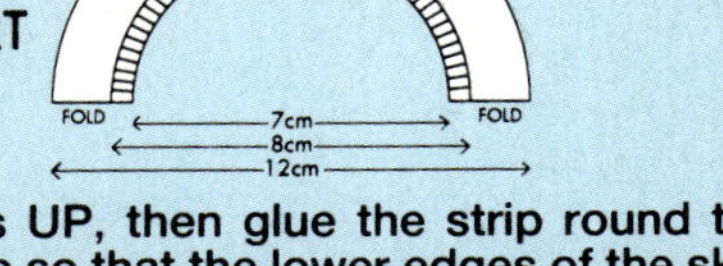

8. Bend the tabs UP, then glue the strip round the bottom of the tube so that the lower edges of the skirt and the tube are level when it stands on the table, ends meeting at the back.
9. Glue a 1 cm wide strip of gift-wrap over the skirt tabs.
10. Cut a piece of gift-wrap 7 x 3 cm for the muff (pink the long edges). Roll up, overlap and stick the short ends. Glue to front of tube, over lower corners of the cape.
11. To make the hair, wind yarn 25-30 times around 20 cm-deep piece of stiff card. Tie the loops at each edge tightly with a single strand of yarn (figure 4), then remove from card and tie the centre *loosely* with another strand (figure 5). Finally, knot the two *end* ties together.

FIGURE 4: HAIR

20cm

FIGURE 5: HAIR

KNOT TIES

12. Rest the egg on top of the tube, then glue the hair round it, the knotted end ties at the back.
13. Draw the features with felt pens, following the illustration for guidance.
14. Make the hats from gift-wrap as follows:

VICTORIAN BONNET: Cut a 15 cm diameter semi-circle of folded gift-wrap and stick the cut edges together. Then curve around the head as illustrated, gluing the corners to the face. Decorate the bonnet and muff with flowers cut from the gift-wrap.

PICTURE HAT: Cover both sides of a 10 cm diameter circle of thin card with 12 cm circles of gift-wrap: trim the overlap with pinking shears. Cut a 4 cm diameter hole in the centre. Glue to the head as illustrated, covering the top of the head, and the muff, with flowers cut from the gift-wrap.

STRIPED TOQUE: Roll up a 4 x 50 cm strip of gift-wrap to make a 4.5 cm diameter tube. Tape the join, then line with wrap. Glue firmly to the top of the head. To make each loop, fold a 4 x 26 cm strip of gift-wrap in half and stick back-to-back. Pink the edges, then curve round and stick the ends together. Fix four loops at the back of the hat, as shown.

Big's Tall

IT all started one afternoon when Bertha's dad decided to water his garden with the hose. I always like to know what's going on, so I trotted over to have a look, and suddenly the water stopped flowing.

Well, to be honest, there WAS a reason, but I hadn't realised what it was. Neither had Dad. He just looked down the hose to see where the water had gone — and then he looked at me.

"Get off the hose, you stupid dog!" he yelled. "No — wait — not yet — SPLURRGGH!"

Too late. I'm a very obedient dog, I always do as Dad yells. Unfortunately, Dad still had the hose pointed at his face when the water started flowing again . . .

Bertha hurried to defend me as Dad, growling, mopped his face.

"Big only did what you told him to, Dad!" she pointed out.

"GRR! That ANIMAL!" roared Dad. "I've HAD it with him! He's USELESS! All he does is get in the way! He lounges around, eats enough for six horses, and doesn't even do a single thing for his keep!"

"What do you expect him to do?" asked Bertha. "He's only a dog, after all!"

She needn't have put it quite like that, but I saw her point. Dad, however, didn't!

"OTHER dogs manage to be useful!" he declared. "Take Labradors, for instance. They fetch things. Last time that great hairy hound of yours fetched my paper, what happened?"

I remembered. Well, it hadn't been my fault. I'd really thought Dad WANTED a nice game of tug o' war. And the paper didn't get VERY torn . . . I mean, MOST of it was left. I only drooled over one end of it, and the fuss he kicked up, you wouldn't believe!

He was still kicking one up now, come to that.

"And guard dogs! They're useful." Dad went on. "They guard things. Does HE guard things? Our house, for instance? Pah! Fat lot of use HE'D be if a burglar tried to break in. Half a biscuit and he's anybody's!"

I thought that was a bit much. Fancy suggesting that I could be bribed by half a biscuit! . . . Mind you, if it was one of those lovely chocolatey ones, the crunchy sort, with the soft bit in the middle . . .

Dad was still fuming.

"Even that Westie next door is more use than Big," he said.

"He catches rats. This dog of yours is SCARED of them!"

Scared of rats? I'LL say I am! They TERRIFY me! Have you ever SEEN a rat? They're HUGE — nasty great things with all these horrible sharp teeth . . . brrr! I'd rather tackle a burglar any day. Specially if he was armed with half a chocolate biscuit.

But I could see Dad was really upset this time, and I decided I'd better do something to cheer him up a bit, and to show him just what an asset I was around the place.

And I knew just how to do it. I've got this bone, you see. I'd buried it somewhere for a special occasion, and THIS was the occasion, I decided! While Dad stomped off indoors to dry himself, I hurried to dig up my bone.

I KNEW roughly where it was buried, so it only took me four or five digging sessions to find it. I had to dig up a few weeds while searching, but it was worth it.

That bone was lovely. It smelt really ripe and had lots of rotten meat and bits of mud clinging to it. I knew Dad wouldn't be able to resist it. Who could?

I carried it indoors and dropped it proudly right where Dad would be sure to find it — on his favourite armchair. What could be nicer than sitting on comfy cushions and

gnawing on a delicious, smelly bone? It's MY favourite way of spending an afternoon.

I trotted back out into the garden, imagining Dad's delighted face when he saw my present on his chair.

Well, you may not believe this, but about two minutes later Dad shot out into the garden, and his face wasn't delighted at all. It was more . . . how shall I describe it? . . . PURPLE. He was holding the bone at arm's length, and holding his nose, too.

"Isn't that Big's bone, Dad?" asked Bertha.

"I KNOW IT IS!" roared Dad. "The great hairy nit tried to bury it in my armch . . ."

He stopped. His eyes bulged. His face turned from purple to white, then green.

"MY LETTUCES!!" he bellowed, pointing at the garden where I'd dug up the bone. "It took me ALL THIS MORNING to plant out those seedlings and that . . . that ANIMAL has dug them all up again! Why, I'll . . ."

I didn't stick around to find out what he'd do. I shot off round the side of the house. My efforts to impress him with my generosity had failed miserably. Though I can't help thinking he shouldn't have planted his weedy little lettuces right where I'd buried my bone.

Still, I had to think up SOME way to impress Dad. But how?

Then I remembered a Dog Show to which Bertha'd once taken me. There'd been lots of impressive dogs there, with impressive titles. (*I* hadn't won any — but that might have been something to do with me knocking over that lady judge. I was only trying to be friendly when I put my paws on her shoulders and licked her face, but people can be hard to fathom out sometimes.)

I recalled the titles. Dog with the Waggiest Tail had been one of them. Now THAT was something I could achieve!

Well — I tried.

And tried.

Not that I'd describe my tail as stumpy, mind you. Just a bit on the short side. But even I have to admit that when I tried wagging it, it just looked like a blur of fur. I didn't think I'd impress Dad that way.

Well, there'd been other titles. Let me see . . . there was The Dog with the Most Soulful Eyes. Now THAT I can do! Humans just can't resist dogs with soulful eyes!

So I went to practise on Bertha, who was sitting on a sunbed, reading.

"Are you all right, Big?" she asked, as I switched my very best soulful look on, full power. "You look sort of funny."

I explained to her that I was looking soulful. "Aroooo!" is how I put it.

"Oh, I get it," said Bertha. "You've got a tummyache. Well, I told you you were eating your dinner too fast."

And that was the end of my soulful look. You know, it's funny how humans just can't speak Dog . . . even the reasonably bright ones, like Bertha.

BUT I wasn't giving up! There had to be SOME way to make Dad see what a bonus to the family I was!

Then I remembered the Best Groomed Dog category. The Best Groomed Dog at the show had really impressed everyone. Now there was my chance! I think I'm a pretty elegant sort of chap at the best of times, if you'll pardon my saying so. With my fur washed and brushed, and my best collar on, I knew I'd make a great impression on Dad.

But I needed Bertha's help for this one. So I hurried to fetch the big tin bath she uses to bathe me, and dragged it across the lawn to her. To give her the idea, I hopped into it and pretended to be washing myself. Her eyes popped.

"You want a BATH, Big?" she gasped. "Crumbs, you MUST be feeling ill!"

I can understand her surprise, to be fair. Normally, when she wants to wash me, I run a mile. She usually has to drag me every

centimetre of the way to the tub, howling. Well, YOU try taking a bath with a thick fur coat on and see how YOU like it. Yugh!

Still, to get round Dad, and make up for my — erm — little mistakes with the hosepipe and the lettuce patch, I'd suffer even that. So she bathed me. And I didn't struggle at all.

And when I was dried and brushed, with my best collar on, I can tell you I looked VERY smart.

Easily the Best Groomed Dog Dad had ever seen, I reckoned. He'd be knocked out. "That's the Best Groomed Dog I've ever seen!" he'd gasp.

I was just going to go and fetch him, to see me in all my glory, when suddenly . . .

That Standard Poodle from next door but one had to go and walk by, didn't it?

Clipped fur. Pretty bow on its head. Diamond-studded collar. Even its TOENAILS were manicured.

And with a sinking heart, I realised I didn't even stand the chance of winning the title of Best Groomed Dog on Our Side of the Street.

So much for me EVER impressing Dad. I suppose he's right, I AM useless. I'm not a guard dog, or a retriever, or a ratter. I'm not well groomed, or waggy. My generosity isn't appreciated and I'm obviously just not the soulful type, either.

I'm a failure. It's hopeless. I'll never . . .

Hey!

Hang on!

Wait a minute!!

I know JUST how to impress Dad!

And what's more — it's something I've ALREADY DONE!!

Want to know what it is? Turn the page upside down!

I WROTE THIS STORY!!

BOBBY DAZZLER
BOBBY DAZZLER was the only girl at Westbury Boarding School for boys, where her mother was matron. Mike Norton and Don Carter spent a lot of their time competing for Bobby's attention. One evening . . .
The boys are having football practice. GREAT! They never mind me joining in.
And so —
That was a brilliant set piece move! We'll be okay if we can pull off a few of them in the match!
What match is this?
Us against Burntwood Boys' School, our big rivals. There's a cup at stake, plus a special man of the match award!
Sounds serious stuff.
It is. That's why there's a vital position we want YOU to be in, Bobby old pal.
Just name it!
Goalie perhaps. I'm quite good at that. Or up front . . .

Behind the goal, cheering us on — as our number one fan!
WHAT?

Come off it, boys! I should be in the team. You *KNOW* I'm good enough.
Westbury include a *GIRL* in their side? We'd be a laughing stock! Buzz off now and leave us to it, there's a good girl!

They're not getting away with speaking to ME like that.

I want to be in the team, sir! Why am I not being considered? Is there some rule that says a girl can't play?
Well . . . no, I don't suppose so . . .

Then I should be in with a chance. You said yourself I'm quite good.
It's true you make a good goalie, and you're reasonable as a forward, too . . .

I know! We'll make you sub. We're only allowed one sub for this match, so it'd be useful to have someone who can play in several positions.
That's pleased her!
Thanks, sir!

We defenders will stick to him like glue, sir.

YEAH! We won't let him *TOUCH* the ball!

Can I see?

Wow! He looks *SUPER!*

Bobby!

Huh! He'll be looking fed up by the time *WE'VE* finished with him and his team!

The next day —

Here we go! Good luck!

I can't see Barry anywhere.

Nor me.

Where's your star striker?
Barry Dobson? Right at the back. He's only playing sub today. He's played so much lately, we decided to rest him for a difficult game. We can beat you lot without risking Barry!

The cheek!
Did you *HEAR* that?
You sit on the bench, Bobby.
Next to Barry! This could be my lucky day!

Hi! How come there's a girl at Westbury?
It's a long story. I'll tell you . . .
It's not that long really, but I'm SURE I can spin it out!
B

. . . and so now I'm one of the lads!
Even getting into the school football team. I'm impressed! What position do you play?

I suppose goalie's my first choice. I'm quite good at that — except when I have to save a low ball to my left. That's my weak spot!

Here come the Burntwood strikers!
How dare that toad Barry chat up OUR sub? I wonder what he's saying to make her laugh so much?

Save it, Mike!
What . . . ? Oh, NO! I've let it in!

Great! We're one up!
You idiot, Mike! You weren't concentrating!
Huh! It's all Bobby's fault! I was watching her and Barry!

The match continued —
It's nearly half-time. Start loosening up, Barry. I might play you in the second half.
Okay, sir.
I'll loosen up, too. Our teacher might decide to play ME.

Have you tried this exercise?
No. Show me how you do it.

Come on, Don!
What on earth are Bobby and Barry doing now?

Missed! You pain! It was an *OPEN* goal!

Half-time and we're a goal down. You'll have to do better than this, lads.
It was Mike's fault. He let the goal in.
Rubbish! Don's to blame. He missed an easy equaliser.

Don't you put the blame on me, Mike! Take that!
AAH!

Are you all right?
Do I look it?
You can't go on in that state. The sub will have to be goalie.
Great! My big chance!

And you're relegated to the sidelines too, my lad. I won't have people who fight in my team — *WHATEVER* the provocation.
But, sir! With Mike *AND* Don off, and only Bobby to replace them — we'll be down to ten men!

You can't even count! You mean *NINE* men and a girl! Just get out there and do your best!

Our two best men gone, and only a *GIRL* to replace them. This is a disaster!
Where *IS* our sub? She's holding up play.

A girl has to get her priorities right! This should do.

On the pitch —
Barry IS playing, and the Burntwood team have possession.

COME ON, BARRY!
SHOOT!
He's aiming low down to my left.

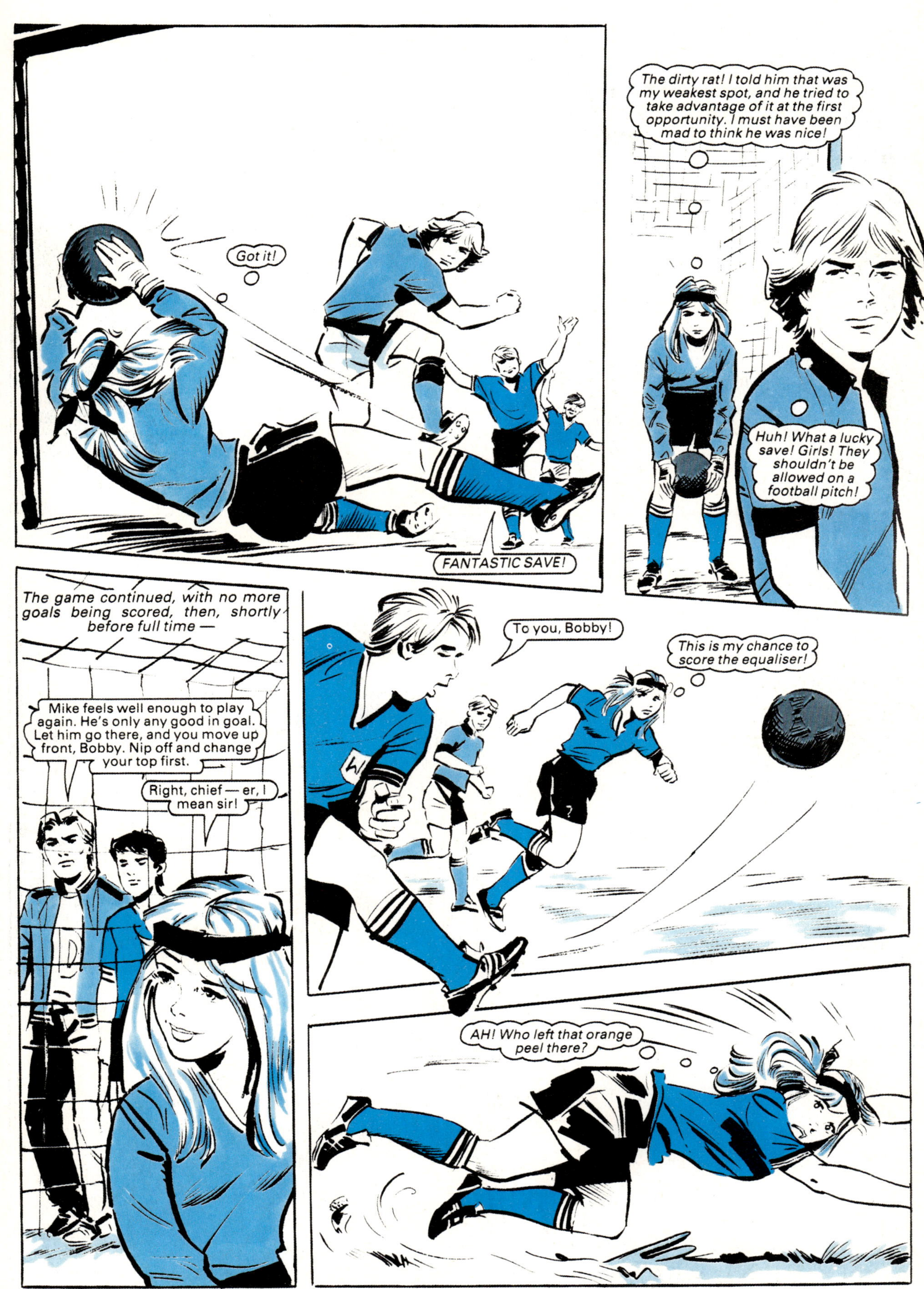
Got it!
FANTASTIC SAVE!
The dirty rat! I told him that was my weakest spot, and he tried to take advantage of it at the first opportunity. I must have been mad to think he was nice!
Huh! What a lucky save! Girls! They shouldn't be allowed on a football pitch!
The game continued, with no more goals being scored, then, shortly before full time —
Mike feels well enough to play again. He's only any good in goal. Let him go there, and you move up front, Bobby. Nip off and change your top first.
Right, chief — er, I mean sir!
To you, Bobby!
This is my chance to score the equaliser!
AH! Who left that orange peel there?

OW!
A header! FANTASTIC!

You scored!
I DID?
And the whistle's blown for full time. It's a draw!

Three cheers for Bobby!
It was a fantastic goal! How did you do it?
I wish I knew!

I am pleased to present this trophy to the player who saved magnificently in goal, and then scored a brilliant equaliser for Westbury. The man of the match award goes to . . . Bobby Dazzler!

Well done, Bobby! They can't present the other cup, though, as it was a draw. So there will have to be a replay. And don't worry — next time YOU'LL be in from the start, Bobby!
Man of the match, AND another whole game to come? What more could a girl ask for?
TIME UP!

JUDY
60s
NIGHT
Hey, that sixties' night looks as though it might be fun!
We went to one on our hols last year, Judy. They played sixties' music, and we all wore sixties' outfits. It was brill!

FAB! That's what they said in the sixties. . . . FABulous!
Let's go! It's tonight.

So that afternoon—
No, we wore our skirts shorter than that, Judy . . .

. . . and really pale lipstick and black eyes!
I think Mum's enjoying this more than me!

There — that's about right! And here's Mandy! You look just right, Mandy!

Thanks for the lift, Dad. Are those boys going in?
No, but who cares? There'll be loads more inside!

But inside—
There's something wrong, here! These people are all ancient!
Oh, no! Remember that poster we saw was a bit torn?

Here's the full version!
OVER 60s
NIGHT
FAB!

Practice Makes Perfect

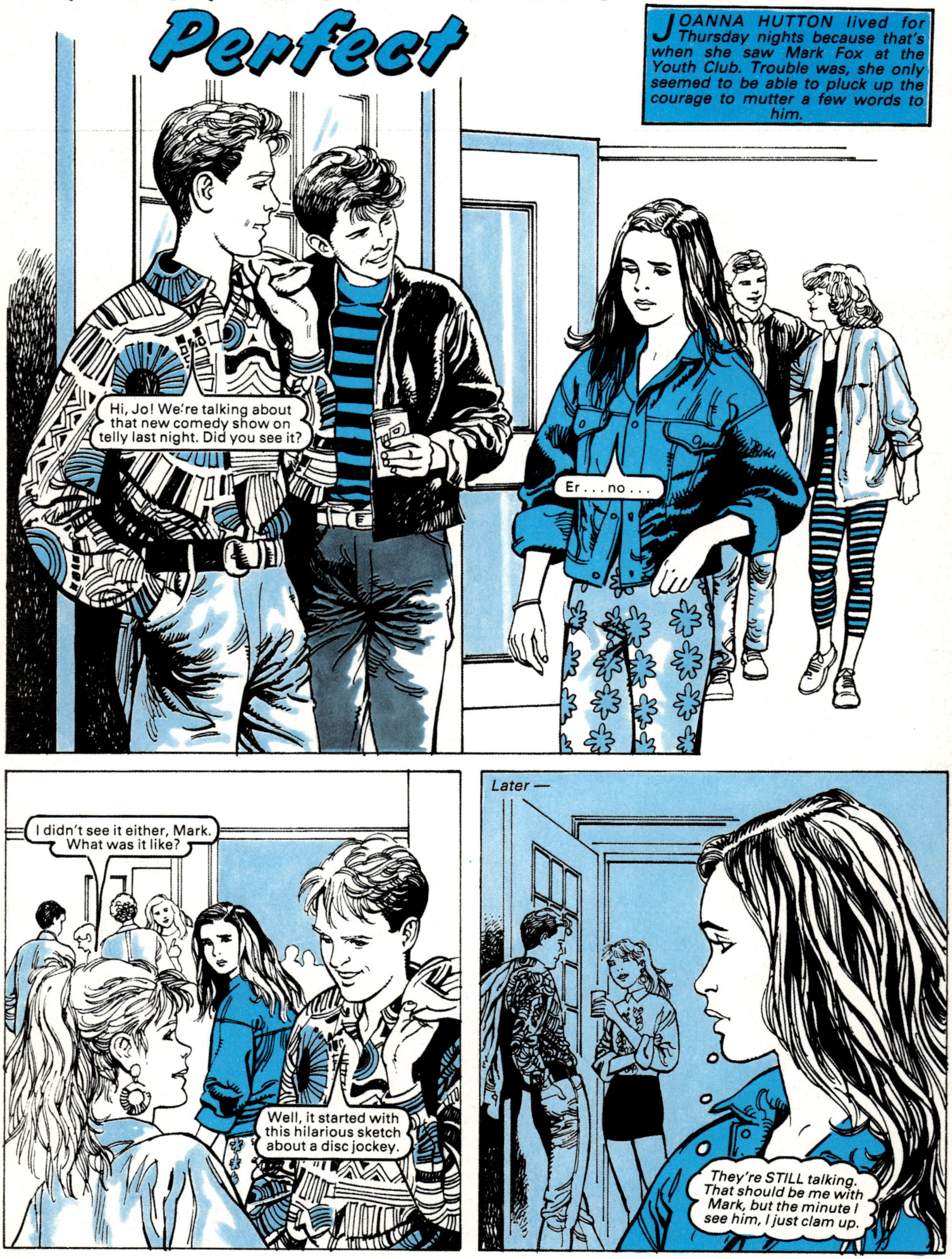

JOANNA HUTTON lived for Thursday nights because that's when she saw Mark Fox at the Youth Club. Trouble was, she only seemed to be able to pluck up the courage to mutter a few words to him.

Hi, Jo! We're talking about that new comedy show on telly last night. Did you see it?

Er . . . no . . .

Joanna was still thinking about her problem on Saturday —
It's because I LIKE Mark that I can't think of anything to say. My throat goes all dry.
And now here's some advice for any viewer who feels that shyness is spoiling life . . .

If your throat dries up and your mind goes a blank as soon as you want to do something important . . .
That's EXACTLY how I am about speaking to Mark!

. . . practise beforehand on someone who ISN'T so important to you. Then when you come to do the real thing, pretend you're STILL practising.

That's what I'll do! I'll practise chatting to some boy I DON'T care about — to build up my confidence for Mark!
Joanna, will you come and help me with the shopping?
Yes, Mum.

And, in the local supermarket —
There's Simon! I'll practise on him! Mum reckons he quite likes me, but I'm not bothered about him — so he's ideal!

This is his dad's shop so he's here all day Saturday — and most evenings after school.

Hi, Simon! I . . . I like your T-shirt.
I got it in that new place in town.

Wow! Joanna managed to keep talking until Mum had done all the shopping —
I must go now. See you again, Simon.
Hey, that was easy!

MARKET
Daily
You just open your mouth and say SOMETHING! It needn't be anything desperately witty!
710
CARDS
I think Joanna likes me! Great!

Each afternoon for the next few days, she called at the shop on the way home from school —
What a terrible afternoon we've had. History — I hate it. French is my favourite.
Got to keep practising.

I love all languages. We might be going to Greece for our holidays.
After all, practice makes perfect!

And on Thursday at the Club —
There's Mark. Now all I've got to do is pretend he's Simon, and it'll be easy to talk to him.

Hi, Joanna!
Hi, Mark. Er . . . I like your jumper. Where did you get it?

My mum made it.
I wish *I* could knit!

She kept chattering, just as she'd practised with Simon, and, at the end of the evening —
Do you fancy coming out with me tomorrow night?
Yeah. Okay.
It's worked! I'll write and tell that woman on the telly she's a genius! I've got a date with Mark!

rant
Burger Bar
Should we go in here?
Yes, fine, Mark.

But, soon —
. . . so normally I play centre forward — but I can turn my hand to most positions. Or should I say, "turn my feet"? Ha! Ha!
Gosh, he might be nice-looking — but he's really boring when you get to know him! He's gone on all night about football and how wonderful he is.

Of course the team just couldn't keep going without me — that's certain.
And big-headed, too! I suppose I didn't notice last night because I was too busy making sure I kept talking to him — pretending he was Simon.

And, suddenly, she realised —
I wish he WERE Simon! I thought Simon didn't mean anything to me — I was just practising on him — but I've REALLY come to like him. I must go back to the shop tomorrow.

So, next day —
CASH
Joanna, you weren't in the shop yesterday. I missed you!

Er . . . er . . . I . . . I . . .
Joanna . . .
Oh, no! My throat's gone all dry!

. . . you're very quiet! Are you all right?
Y-yes.
The only problem is, now I KNOW it's Simon I like, I can't think of a thing to say to him!
The End

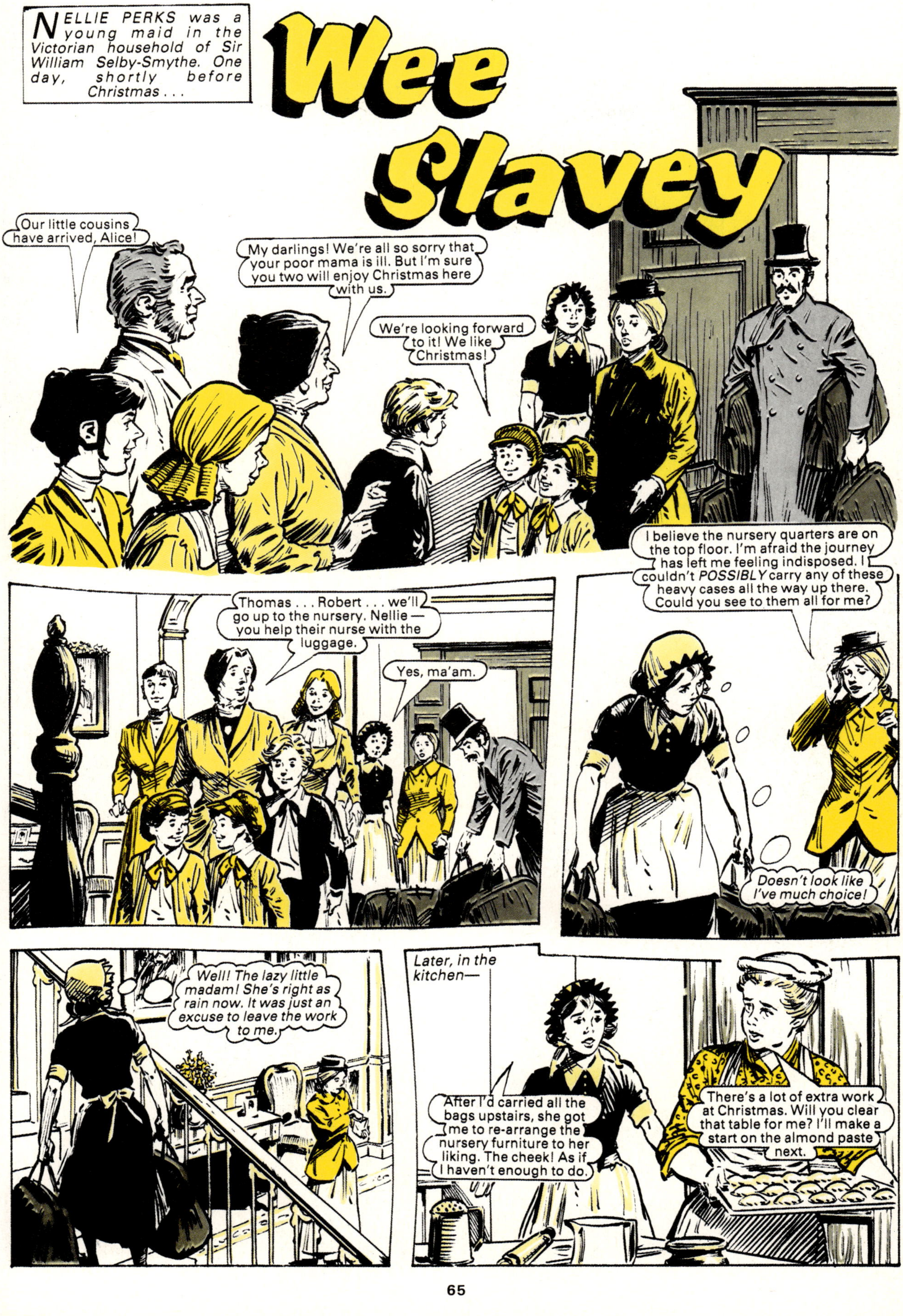

Wee Slavey

Our little cousins have arrived, Alice!

My darlings! We're all so sorry that your poor mama is ill. But I'm sure you two will enjoy Christmas here with us.

We're looking forward to it! We like Christmas!

Thomas . . . Robert . . . we'll go up to the nursery. Nellie — you help their nurse with the luggage.

Yes, ma'am.

I believe the nursery quarters are on the top floor. I'm afraid the journey has left me feeling indisposed. I couldn't *POSSIBLY* carry any of these heavy cases all the way up there. Could you see to them all for me?

Doesn't look like I've much choice!

E

Then—
Oh no! There's the drawing room bell. NOW what?
You rang, ma'am.
More work!
Yes. We want you to clear a space in the corner for the Christmas tree.
Look a bit more excited, Nellie! It's not Christmas without a tree.
All the IMPORTANT people have one — from royalty downwards. It was Prince Albert who first started the custom, you know. I think it's absolutely thrilling!
Huh! Miss Flora and Miss Alice might not be so keen if they were the ones who had to go humping furniture around to fit it in.
TRA-LA!
Oh, William! It's beautiful!
It's the largest tree we've ever had! I hope it's bigger than the Wilson-Burkes'. The one they had last year was positively gigantic.
Can we decorate it? PLEASE!
Calm down, boys. Certainly you may decorate the tree. Here are the baubles.
If you'd just give me a hand with it, Nellie.

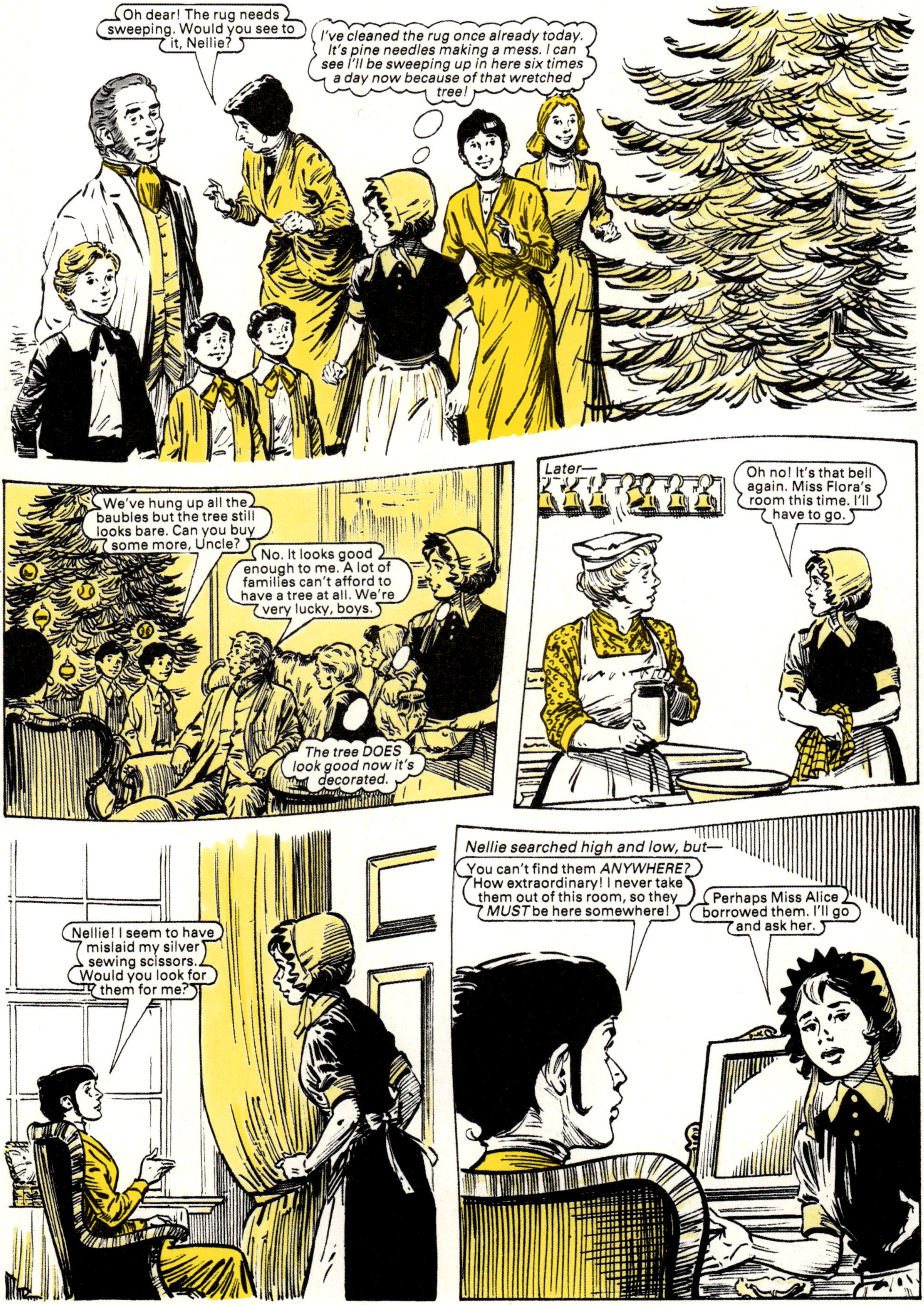

Oh dear! The rug needs sweeping. Would you see to it, Nellie?

I've cleaned the rug once already today. It's pine needles making a mess. I can see I'll be sweeping up in here six times a day now because of that wretched tree!

We've hung up all the baubles but the tree still looks bare. Can you buy some more, Uncle?

No. It looks good enough to me. A lot of families can't afford to have a tree at all. We're very lucky, boys.

The tree DOES look good now it's decorated.

Later—

Oh no! It's that bell again. Miss Flora's room this time. I'll have to go.

Excuse me, please. I wish to get to Miss Alice's room.
Oh — sorry.
What's the nurse hanging round for? She's supposed to be looking after the twins, not gazing out of the windows.
In Miss Alice's room—
No, Nellie, I haven't borrowed my sister's scissors — but I have lost something, too. My brass belt buckle has gone missing. Do you know where it is?
I'm afraid not, Miss Alice.
Much later—
I've been searching for things the young ladies lost — and I didn't find them! Now I'm even MORE behind with my work.
Perhaps the nurse would help you. Sir William has taken the boys for a ride in his carriage, so she must be at a loose end. Ask her if she'll prepare the little lads' tea.
But—
Certainly not! Kitchen slaving is YOUR job. Besides, I'm going out now. I've an aunt who lives near here and I'm taking the opportunity to deliver a Christmas present to her.
Huh! I wish I had time for visiting.
Nellie! The flowers in the drawing room are past their best. Kindly remove them.
Yes, ma'am.
There's not a moment's peace!
Still, it's nice to see the tree again. It looks so sparkling and beautiful now it's been decorated. I was silly to be cross when it first arrived.

Later—
Did the boys enjoy their carriage trip, sir?
I think so. They certainly tired *ME* out!
Here comes that nurse, back at last.
My goodness! Where did you get that hat? You weren't wearing it when you left.
It was a Christmas present from my aunt.
It looks expensive. Her aunt must be rich.
Next day—
That's odd! Two of the silver teaspoons are missing — *AND* a silver napkin ring's disappeared too!
Well don't look at me! I haven't borrowed them! They'll turn up. I expect you put them back in the wrong place what with being so busy.
But, that afternoon—
I wish to wear my gold bracelet when Sir William and I visit the Cardew-Browns this evening. It's in that box, Nellie. Kindly fetch it.
Yes, ma'am.
OH!
The bracelet's not here, ma'am.
WHAT?
My daughters both mislaid things yesterday. Frankly, I put it down to their carelessness. But, now that I have lost something too, I can come to only one conclusion — there is a *THIEF* at work in this house!
Oh, lawks! Maybe that explains the missing spoons and napkin ring.

Lady Smythe called a meeting of the servants—
I now know that at least six items have been taken. Obviously the thief is not a member of the family, so it must be one of the staff. Either the culprit owns up by tomorrow, or I shall have no alternative but to dismiss you all!
Tomorrow is Christmas Eve! It's going to be a rotten Christmas if we're all out of a job.
Who can the thief be, Nellie?
There's only one possible person! That lazy nurse! I saw her hanging around by the bedrooms, then she left the house carrying a small parcel and came back with an expensive new hat! I don't think she visited an aunt. I think she stole the items, sold them, and used the money to buy herself that hat!
The little madam! We could lose our jobs because of her.
Not if I can help it! I'll go and find her and see if I can persuade her to own up.
But—
The twins are running riot in the nursery, but there's no sign of the nurse. She wasn't in her sitting room either. Maybe the drawing room . . .
However—
No sign of her here! Oh, the tree does look nice! It seems to look brighter and sparkle more every time I see it now.
Of course! THAT'S it!

Just then—
Nellie! Do you wish to own up to the thefts?
I'm no thief, ma'am. But I know where the missing items are.
Where?
Right in front of you — hanging on the Christmas tree!
WHAT?
WHERE?
Look carefully and you'll see them all — the brass buckle, the silver scissors, spoons and napkin ring, and the gold bracelet. They've been hanging on the tree all the time!
Oh, yes!
But *WHO* would do that?
I can guess!
And so—
Little terrors! Still, I can't feel too cross with Thomas and Robert. It's that nurse's fault. She should take more care of them. She's a lazy thing but she's not dishonest! It's a good job I realised the truth in time.
Of course it was us! We wanted some more decorations for the tree. Uncle wouldn't buy any, so we found some ourselves!
Shall we untie the things, Mama?
No. Leave them on until after Christmas. The tree looks so nice as it is.
I agree! It's beautiful. And it *IS* bigger than the Wilson-Burkes' tree. I checked when I was round there yesterday. It's the best tree in the whole street!
I wouldn't know about that. But one thing's for sure, it's certainly the most unusual!
THE END

A DOG IS

The new puppy was cute and appealing — but could it take the place of Laura's beloved Bess?

FOR LIFE...

"WHAT a sweet little puppy!" exclaimed Laura's mother, as Uncle Simon brought the fluffy young dog into the room. "Oh, Laura! Isn't he gorgeous?"

Laura looked up from where she was sitting by the big hearth, tickling the tummy of her Old English Sheepdog, Bess. There was a time when Bess had looked just like this puppy. But that was long ago.

"He's for you!" Uncle Simon grinned. "After all, Bess is getting old now, and —"

"No!" shouted Laura angrily. "No!"

Uncle Simon was just the same as her parents, continually reminding her that an old dog like Bess couldn't go on for ever, and expecting Laura to replace her precious Bess with some other animal. As if any other dog could possibly take Bess's place!

Still fuming, Laura jumped to her feet, called Bess, and went out with her into the farm yard. She didn't even want to stay in the same room as that stupid puppy!

From the yard, Laura and Bess took the meadow route, down past the old duck pond and on to the stile. And all the while Laura's thoughts were on Bess and how things had been long ago . . .

Laura had been little more than a toddler when Uncle Simon had first presented her with Bess. He and Auntie Anne bred Old English Sheepdogs on the smallholding they owned which adjoined Laura's parents' farm.

"She'll make a fine companion for the lass," Uncle Simon had smiled.

Laura had jumped up and down excitedly, watching as the sweet little puppy bounded around their old farmhouse kitchen, falling over its great big feet and chasing round excitedly after its own tail. She'd fallen in love with Bess immediately.

Laura and Bess had grown up together — with Bess the only friend Laura had ever wanted. It was a good thing really. Other children Laura's age were few and far between in the isolated countryside that was her home.

Laura remembered how the two of them had shared secret picnics together; how Bess had snuggled up beside her in the den she'd made in the hollow trunk of the old oak tree, and how they'd paddled together in the shallow waters of the farm duck pond. Even in the height of summer those murky waters had seemed icy to Laura, but Bess had loved it — bounding back and forth to fetch sticks her mistress threw. Oh, happy days!

The years had passed quickly. Soon Laura was starting at the tiny village infant school, then bussing to the nearby town for juniors, then seniors. Now she wasn't an excited toddler any more, but a lively thirteen-year-old girl.

But time hadn't been so kind to Bess. Though only ten years old, she was — in human terms — an old lady now. No longer did she bound about excitedly or rush around in circles to chase her own tail. Instead, she walked slowly and carefully, the expression on her face revealing the aches she felt in her old bones, and Laura knew that the days they would share together were numbered.

But that didn't mean she wanted that stupid puppy to take Bess's place — or any other dog, come to that. No. When her beloved Bess went, Laura would be alone. That was the way she wanted it, she'd decided. For her, it was Bess — or nothing!

Laura glanced at her watch as they approached the stile. The evening paper should have arrived by now. Laura's parents' farm was so far out of the village that the paper boy had a tradition whereby he didn't cycle all the way to the farmhouse, but left the paper at the base of the stile for Laura and Bess to come and collect.

Sure enough, the folded paper lay waiting on the ground.

"Up, Bess!" Laura called, urging the old dog up onto the first rung of the stile, to scramble over and collect the paper as she had done for years.

In the early days it had been an easy task for the sprightly animal. A bound to the first rung, then a leap over, where she picked up the paper in her mouth and then jumped back again with it.

Lately, though, Bess had been finding it more difficult, until — just recently — Laura had had to place her hand under the animal to help her up. She put her hand down now to do this. But it was no good.

Even with her mistress's helping hand, Bess couldn't make it. She tried once, then again and again, until it almost broke Laura's heart to see her.

"Never mind, old girl," she whispered at last. "You stay here. *I'll* climb the stile for the paper."

BESS looked worn out by the time they arrived back at the farmhouse.

"You have a rest by the fire," Laura told her gently.

But, when she opened the door, she was annoyed to see that silly puppy still there — sitting in the middle of the hearth rug.

Seeing Laura and Bess walk in, he jumped up and ran excitedly over to them, his tail wagging nineteen to the dozen and his big feet slipping on the polished tile floor. But Laura ignored him.

"Why is *he* still here?" she asked crossly.

"Uncle Simon left him in case you changed your mind," her mother replied. "Really, Laura, it's very unkind of you to refuse your uncle's gift."

"It'd be more unkind to take an animal I don't want!" Laura retorted. "You're always saying that, Mum — that people who don't really want animals shouldn't have them, Well *I* don't want *him*."

Laura meant it too. The puppy's energy, his youth, his vitality — all the things her uncle had hoped would attract her to him, only made her hate him more, because they brought home to her the fact that poor, dear Bess wasn't like

that any more. Poor Bess was old and ailing.

Laura fed Bess and Mum fed the puppy. Then, after supper, the family settled down for an evening in front of the fire — that stupid puppy cuddling up to Bess for company and warmth. How dare he take even an inch of the fireside space that rightly belonged to her beloved Bess? Laura watched him angrily.

Then suddenly the stockman came in, talking anxiously about an emergency outside. It seemed one of the cows was calving and things weren't going smoothly. Both Laura's parents rushed off to the barn.

"You'll be all right with the dogs," Laura's mother called as they hurried out.

Dogs! Huh! Laura didn't want to be with the *dogs.* She wanted to be with just one dog — Bess. And why shouldn't she be? That puppy could sleep outside, in one of the sheds!

She wasn't being cruel, Laura told herself, as she took the whimpering creature outside. There were lots of dogs on the farm — border collies her father used for working the sheep, and a big Alsatian they had as a guard dog — and they all slept outside. It was only Bess, who was a pet, who was allowed in the house.

Laura settled the puppy with an elderly border collie she knew would take good care of it. Let him be a farm dog if her parents insisted he stayed, she thought. Then, happily, she went inside again to her beloved Bess.

Laura's mother wasn't too pleased the next morning when she found the puppy had spent the night in the shed, even if he had been warm and comfortable out there. But she was even more angry when Laura got Bess up for her afternoon walk and pointedly left the puppy behind.

"He needs exercise too," she called crossly. "Take him too."

Laura looked at her mother's angry face, and knew she had no choice.

"All right, I'll take you," she muttered crossly to the puppy. "But I don't have to *like* you!"

Bess was panting heavily by the time they reached the stile.

"It's all right old girl, you don't have to try and jump over," Laura told her. "I'll fetch the paper."

But Bess determinedly pushed her aside. She positioned herself at the bottom of the stile. The puppy, curious, followed her and started to sniff around excitedly.

Then suddenly, to Laura's amazement, Bess picked the little creature up in her mouth and dropped him gently through the bars of the stile to the other side.

THE puppy looked surprised. Then his eyes caught sight of the folded newspaper. What was this? Something exciting to play with, he was sure!

Excitedly, he grappled with it, taking one end in his mouth. But then, before he could do any damage to it, Bess leaned her head through the stile again, picked him up by the scruff of his neck in her mouth, and skilfully and carefully brought both puppy and paper back through the bars!

Once he was safely back on her side, Bess took the paper from the puppy's mouth and proudly handed it over to Laura. Both dogs wagged their tails excitedly at her — obviously very pleased about what they'd done.

Tears filled Laura's eyes as she bent to take the paper from Bess.

"You're teaching him your old trick," she whispered softly. "Almost as if you . . .

She stopped, unable to finish saying what she was thinking.

Bess nuzzled up to Laura's legs and wagged her tail again, as if understanding what her mistress had almost said — and agreeing.

"I always said no other dog could take your place," Laura whispered softly to Bess. "But perhaps if *you* can accept him, I should learn to, as well. I do believe you want me to have this puppy."

Bess wagged her tail again, and the puppy jumped up at Laura's legs excitedly.

"Down!" she said firmly. "You're all muddy. If I am going to keep you, I'll have to train you."

And before she could do that, Laura knew she would have to give him a name . . .

"Is that puppy sleeping with the collie again tonight?" Laura's mother asked later, as they cleared away the supper things.

"No. Sammi's staying in here from now on," Laura replied. "Bess wants him to — and I do, too."

Laura's mother watched in delighted amazement as Laura slipped on her boots and took both dogs out for an evening walk. What had come over her daughter?

Stopping by the duck pond, Laura idly threw a stick into the water. Bess didn't attempt to run after it. The icy water was too cold for her old bones these days, but Sammi bounded off excitedly to retrieve it.

It was a big stick for such a little puppy, and it looked for a moment as though he might not be able to bring it back to Laura. But Bess waited at the water's edge, to help him drag it out, and then showed him how to return it to his mistress — sitting obediently afterwards for the doggy choc drop Laura always offered for a job well done.

Laura looked down at excited little Sammi. Yesterday she'd been totally disinterested in him, but today . . . today, he seemed quite sweet and appealing!

She liked him, she knew now. Because Bess liked him. Hadn't Bess shown her, by her actions, that she wanted this fellow to take her place after she had gone?

Laura smiled down at the old dog.

"All the years of happiness we've shared together would count for nothing if I ignored your last wish," she said seriously.

Bess wagged her tail. It was as if she knew that by helping Laura to accept a replacement, Bess had made the inevitable parting easier for her young mistress to bear . . .

New Year Resolution

Ooh! Brothers! Scram, you horror!

On New Year's Eve —
Sorry, but I think I've accidentally thrown that party invitation in the fire.
What? But I need that to get into the hotel. Everyone's got an invitation to stop gate-crashers.

What am I going to do?
Calm down! Is this what you're looking for?

You should see your face! It's so red I can warm my hands on it!
Ooh, I get it! Another one of your stupid tricks.

I'll file my nails while the bath's filling.

But then —
Who's left the bath running? There's water all over the bathroom floor.
Oh, no!

Eh? It's only half-full.

Ooh! Benny! I hate you!

Later, at the party —
Great! Paul Collins is here.
I invited him 'specially 'cos I know you fancy him.
It's true, I do. Trouble is, he never seems to notice me.

Much later —
Paul hasn't spoken to me once. He's been chatting to his mates all night.

Yum! Sausage rolls. I know what you're thinking. But tomorrow I'm going on a diet. I know I'm much too fat. That's my New Year Resolution — to lose weight. Have you made any resolutions, Karen?
I hadn't thought about it.

Now that you mention it though, it's not a bad idea. My kid brother's always making up stories to wind me up. In future, I shan't believe a word he says!
Good on you!

And so, on the first day of the year —
Karen! Disaster! Rover's lost!
Oh yeah?
Here we go again . . .

Lost, is he? So how come I can see him asleep under the table?
Bah!

Then, half an hour later —
Where have you been?
Out in the garden. Karen, there's a boy there. Paul Collins, I think his name is.
Paul's come to see ME?

No, of course he hasn't. Calm down, Karen. It's just another silly story.
You must think I'm green, Benny. As if dishy Paul would come and visit ME.

But he has! He's waiting outside.
Yeah, yeah. You go out and speak to him then. Tell him I'm not interested. I'm going upstairs.

But —
It looks like snow. Oh no! Paul IS here. He's walking up the road away from our house. This time Benny WAS telling the truth after all!

And I told him to tell Paul I wasn't interested. I have to do something — and fast!

Paul! Hang on a minute!
Karen! Hello.

I'm really sorry about that message I sent just now. When my brother said you'd come round to see me, I thought he was lying. That's why I said to tell you I wasn't interested. But I am really. I fancy . . .
Eh?

I HAVEN'T been round to see you. I didn't even know you lived in this road. I'm just here delivering leaflets.

Benny WAS just telling another of his stories. I've made an utter fool of myself!

But —
Don't be embarrassed, Karen. I'm glad you spoke out. The truth is, I've fancied YOU for ages too — but I was too shy to say anything. I was afraid you'd give me the brush off.

But now I know you won't, I don't mind asking you out. Will you come to the pictures with me tonight?
I'd love to, Paul. Thanks!

As they turned back for home, Amy arrived —
I've come to see Karen.
Oh — you're visiting the sick.

What do you mean?
Karen's laid up in bed. She slipped on the ice coming home from your party last night and broke her leg.

Hi, Amy!
Karen! But Benny just said you'd broken your leg . . .

Ooh — you pest! It was a stupid lie.
What if it was? It fooled you!

What a pain he is! You must hate having a brother like that, Karen.
Oh — I don't know. He's not so bad really.
Benny certainly did me a good turn today — even though he doesn't realise it!
The End

DOGGIE TAILS!

Cat-astrophes!
OKAY! LET'S SEE YOU CHASE THAT ONE!
QUICKLY! GIVE HIM A JAB WHILE HE STILL THINKS HE'S YOUR FRIEND.
VET
THERE! FINISHED! MUM SAID I'VE TO BRUSH KITTY EVERY DAY TO AVOID PROBLEMS WITH HER HAIRS.
WE'LL CALL HIM CACTUS!
STOP IT, SUSIE. MRS BROWN IS JUST BORROWING YOUR PLATE!
WHY CAN'T YOU FOLLOW PUSSY'S EXAMPLE AND STAY CLEAN AND TIDY?

MARTA'S MARKET STALL

Phew! What a crush! If there are any Victorian cages of birds here they'll go to these dealers. I might as well go home.
Oops! I'm going to be run over by a wardrobe! I'll get out of the way.
Marta went in search of an attendant —
The junk in there? It's waiting to be cleared by the rag and bone man after the sale. Slip me a couple of quid, and you can take what you like.
Done!
Now THIS stuff is more my style! Some folk would call it junk, but not my customers. There's a bird! It's only a moth-eaten parrot. Maybe Miss Cuthbert's drama group could improvise.
Soon —
I don't know if this bird will do, but at least I got some stock for my stall. I'll call on Miss Cuthbert on my way home, and see what she thinks.

And so —
A . . . a parrot! But how did you know? Oh! Is . . . is someone playing a joke on me?
A JOKE? Of course not!
LOOK! That's Charlie. He . . . he belonged to my dear mother. I looked after her here until she passed on. Charlie knows he can scare me, but I can't find anyone to take him. He . . . he had just pecked me when you arrived with that stuffed one!
Charlie, too, had seen the stuffed parrot —
I'd better take this away. I'll go on searching for the kind you want, Miss Cuthbert.
Oh dear! He's angry! He makes SUCH a noise!
That Saturday —
A stuffed parrot! Strange how people like stuffed things. I was up at Castle House yesterday. The place is full of stuffed creatures. Old Mrs Murchison's late husband was a taxidermist.
A man who stuffs animals? Aunt Laura, did she have any birds? Little stuffed birds, in cages?
I do believe she had, but the old lady never lets anything out of the house. She's very lonely since her husband died, but won't even have a cat or a dog for company . . . says they'd trip her up.
That gives me an idea! It's risky, but this could help TWO people.
And so, later —
A cage for Charlie? Well, yes, he has a cage, Marta, but Mother didn't like to see him in it. He loved her, you see. He sat on her shoulder or her chair. He misses her, like I do.
Does he talk?

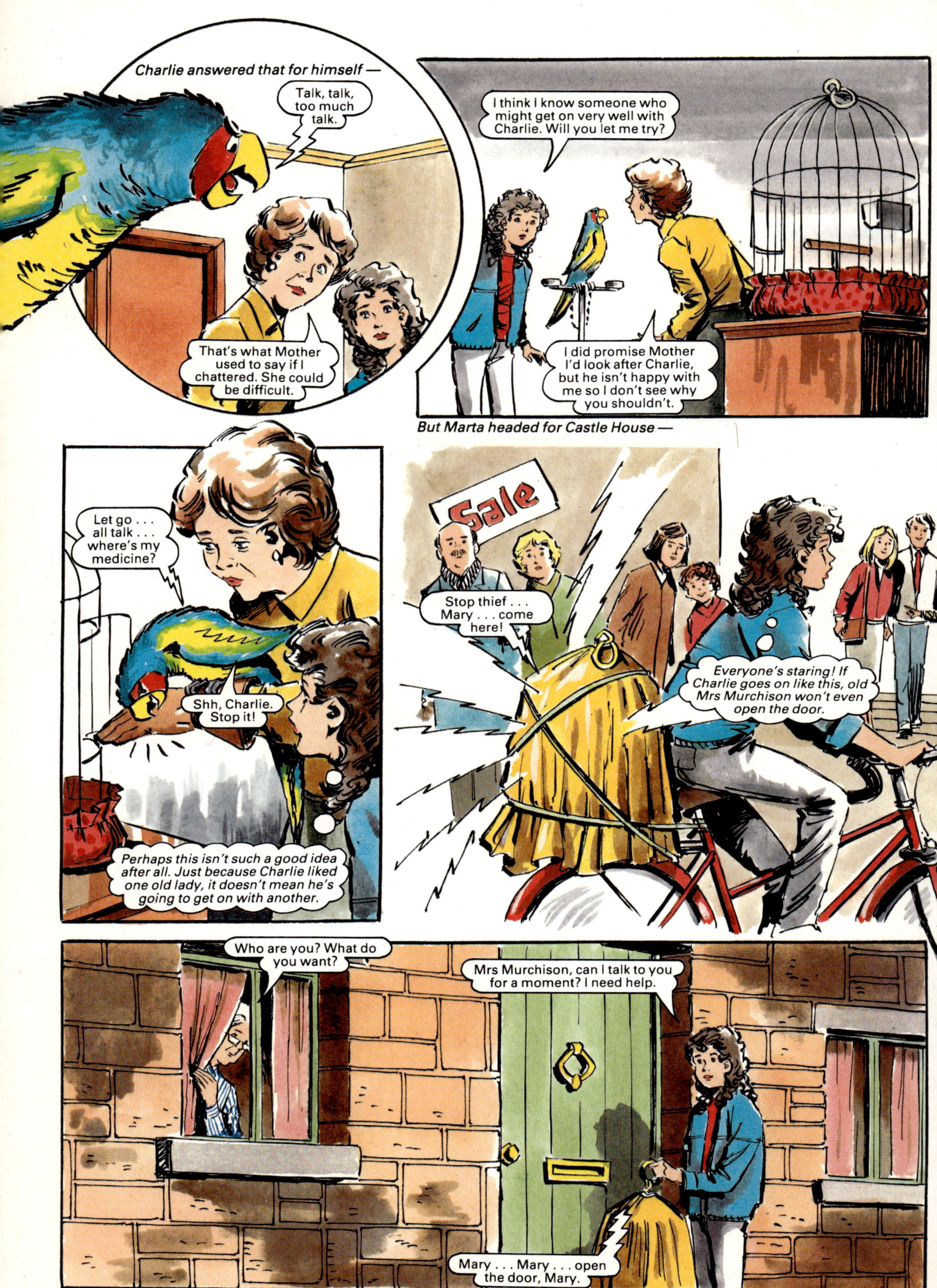
Charlie answered that for himself —
Talk, talk, too much talk.
That's what Mother used to say if I chattered. She could be difficult.
I think I know someone who might get on very well with Charlie. Will you let me try?
I did promise Mother I'd look after Charlie, but he isn't happy with me so I don't see why you shouldn't.
But Marta headed for Castle House —
Let go . . . all talk . . . where's my medicine?
Shh, Charlie. Stop it!
Perhaps this isn't such a good idea after all. Just because Charlie liked one old lady, it doesn't mean he's going to get on with another.
Sale
Stop thief . . . Mary . . . come here!
Everyone's staring! If Charlie goes on like this, old Mrs Murchison won't even open the door.
Who are you? What do you want?
Mrs Murchison, can I talk to you for a moment? I need help.
Mary . . . Mary . . . open the door, Mary.

How did you know?
Know? Know WHAT Mrs Murchison? I . . . er . . . my aunt said she thought you might like company, and . . . well . . . I had an idea.
Mary . . . Charlie loves Mary.
Mary's my name . . . and my husband was called Charlie. Can I take him out of his cage?
Yes . . . that's why I came. Charlie needs a home and I thought perhaps you needed a friend.
But the names were pure chance . . . maybe chance is on my side.
My dear, I HAVE been lonely. These stuffed creatures are all memories of my dear Charlie at work. But I have been getting a little silly about them. Yes, you can borrow those birds. Keep them, in fact. I don't need them now.
Thank you. And . . . and I think a lady would like to visit you as well, when she has time to spare from her dramatic group.
So, a week later —
The play's going well. Miss Cuthbert's done a great job with the props. No-one is lonely any more, and I'll have something unusual for my market stall when the play is over. Great!
THE END

TREATS FOR HA
Thinking of having a Hallowe'en party this year? Then why not try making some of these yummy recipes? They'll make your party the most popular in the street.
SPOOKY ORANGE PUNCH
HALLOWE'EN DREAM PIE
GHOSTLY DESSERT
WITCHES BREW
MIDNIGHT TREAT
HORROR FUDGE CRUNCH
ALWAYS ask an adult before using kitchen equipment.

LOWE'EN!

SPOOKY ORANGE PUNCH

¾ pints (1 litre) prepared Bird's Orange Apeel
½ pint (300 ml.) lemonade
uice of 1 orange
ruit to serve, i.e. apple and orange slices

. Stir together the Orange Apeel, lemonade nd orange juice.

. Chill well and serve in a jug and tall glasses ecorated with fruit slices.

GHOSTLY DESSERT

Bird's Tangerine Sugar Free Jelly
3 oz. (75 g.) digestive biscuits
½ oz. (25 g.) butter
Bird's Sugar Free Angel Delight, any flavour
½ pint (300 ml.) cold milk

. Make up the Sugar Free Jelly as directed on he sachet. Pour into a serving dish and chill vell until set (about 4 hours).

2. Meanwhile crush the digestive biscuits. Melt he butter in a small saucepan and stir in the iscuit crumbs until evenly coated. Leave to ool.

3. When the jelly is completely set, make up he Angel Delight as directed on the sachet nd pour over the jelly.

4. Sprinkle the Angel Delight with the biscuit rumb mixture. If liked, serve decorated with wirls of cream or Dream Topping.

HORROR FUDGE CRUNCH

1 tablespoon (1 x 15 ml. spoon) golden syrup
A small knob of butter
1 oz. (25 g.) cornflakes
1 sachet Bird's Fudge Instant Whip
¾ pint (425 ml.) cold milk
1 fudge bar

1. Heat the syrup and butter in a small saucepan. Stir in the cornflakes until evenly coated. Leave to cool.

2. Make up the Instant Whip as directed on the sachet.

3. Cut the fudge bar into small pieces and stir into the Instant Whip.

4. Divide between four serving dishes. Just before serving sprinkle each glass with the cornflake mixture.

WITCHES BREW

½ pint (300 ml.) cold milk
3 teaspoons (3 x 5 ml. spoons) Bird's Banana Angel Delight
1 banana
1 scoop vanilla ice cream

1. Pour the milk into a blender or liquidiser. Add all the other ingredients and blend for thirty seconds.

2. Pour into tall glasses and serve immediately.

MIDNIGHT TREAT

1 sachet Bird's Strawberry Angel Delight
½ pint (300 ml.) cold milk
2 chocolate flakes
5 fl. oz. (150 ml.) carton natural or strawberry yogurt

1. Make up the Angel Delight as directed on the sachet.

2. Crumble the chocolate flakes and stir most of the chocolate pieces into the Angel Delight reserving some for decoration.

3. Divide the Angel Delight between four serving dishes.

4. Carefully spoon a layer of yogurt over the Angel Delight and serve sprinkled with the remaining chocolate flake.

HALLOWE'EN DREAM PIE

4 oz. (100 g.) plain chocolate
2 oz. (50 g.) cornflakes
1 sachet Bird's Dream Topping
¼ pint (150 ml.) cold milk
1 sachet Bird's Strawberry Angel Delight
½ pint (300 ml.) cold milk

1. Have ready a 7-8 inch (18-20 cm.) loose bottom cake tin.

2. Melt the chocolate gently in a basin over hot water and stir in the cornflakes until evenly coated.

3. Spoon the mixture into the cake tin, press well to the base and sides and put to chill.

4. Make up the Dream Topping as directed on the sachet, and spoon it evenly inside the chocolate case. Put to chill.

5. When nearly ready to serve, make up the Angel Delight as directed on the sachet and swirl into the prepared case.

Cinderella JONES

CINDY JONES worked hard for her keep at the Happyholme Guest House, Brightsea, owned by her stepmother, while her Step-sisters, Isobelle and Sarah, did nothing. It was New Year's Eve and Cindy's father, a travelling salesman, had just arrived home.

But Mr Jones' pleas fell on deaf ears—

WHAT? But I could never afford . . .
Exactly! So Cindy stays HERE tonight — for the good of Happyholme.

So, later—
Huh! Just about everyone in Brightsea is going to tonight's ball — except ME! What I need is a fairy godmother to appear suddenly and make things happen for me.

Just then—
Oh, Cindy! Can I have a cup of tea please?
Certainly, Mrs Bamford.
Well someone's appeared, but it isn't a fairy godmother. Mrs Bamford is a widow who's staying at Happyholme for a few days.

I'm SO miserable. I'd planned to go to tonight's ball with my daughter, Moira. I even hired a ball gown and matching accessories for her. Now the little minx has gone off to a disco on the pier and abandoned me. I don't want to go to the ball alone.

I know! Why don't YOU come with me?
ME?
It's my dream come true!

Wait a minute! There are one or two snags. To start with, I've nothing to wear and the shops are closed now.
You're about the same size as Moira. YOU can wear the hired gown. I'll fetch it!

It's beautiful! But what about the guest house? I can't go and leave the place unattended. Stepmother would be furious.
I'll take over! I've always wanted to be a receptionist!

Thank you, Mrs Leyton.
It's all arranged then. I'll change now. We'll go in my car.

And so—
Nearly there. If we get separated, be sure to meet me in the car park at midnight. I don't like late nights, so I'll go without you if you're not there, and you'll lose your lift home.
I don't see us being separated. Mrs Bamford wanted me to come to keep her company, so I can hardly wander off and leave her.

But, soon—
What a lovely dress you're wearing.
Oh, thank you, kind sir!

There's no need for you to hang around, Cindy dear. Go off and enjoy yourself.
That sounded more like an order than a suggestion. I think Mrs Bamford quite fancies the Major.

Then—
Hi! Are you all alone? How about a dance? My name's Gerry.
Great! Thanks!

Gerry's a handsome guy. Oh-oh! There are Stepmother and the girls. They look furious. I'd better put their minds at rest.

Don't worry about Happyholme. I left it in good hands. I . . . er . . . took on a temporary receptionist.

They still look angry. I can't think why.
Phew! All this dancing's making me thirsty. I'll fetch us drinks.
Thanks!

How *COULD* you?
EH?
Take no notice. The young man you're dancing with is Harry Willsden's son. Agnes and the girls are green with envy!

Gerry — the son of a millionaire? I'd no idea! And he's really nice, too.
There we are. I've brought us some food, too.
Thanks, Gerry.

Time slipped by quickly—
HAPPY NEW YEAR
Oh no! The first stroke of midnight. I daren't miss my lift!
I have to go!

It isn't safe to walk home alone at this time of night, and I must get back before Stepmother. She'll be angry if she finds I left Mrs Leyton in charge. Oh! These shoes! They were okay for dancing, but they're hopeless for running!

That's better! I've taken them off.

HOTEL PARKING ONLY
Here I am, Mrs Bamford!
Just in time, Cindy.
What a fabulous night!

But, next morning—
The dress is all ready to go back to the hire shop. Oh, NO! There's only ONE shoe!

I must have dropped it when I was running. I'd better go back to the hotel and search in the car park.

And where are YOU going? There's work to be done, my girl!
I won't be long, Stepmother.
You CAN'T go out! Mother has a whole list of chores for you to do.
Yes. A list.
Just wait a minute while I see who's at the door.
Oh! M-Mr Willsden!
It's Gerry!
I just wanted to return this shoe . . . oh! What a vision of beauty!
He means ME! He's going to ask me to marry him, then we'll live happily ever after — just like in the fairy tale! No more drudgery for me! I'll live a life of luxury from now on!

What's your name — you gorgeous creature?
Moira Bamford.
EH?

Thanks for the shoe. They were hired for me, though someone else borrowed them last night.
Thank goodness she did. And thank goodness she lost one, too — or I'd never have met YOU!

Smile, Cindy! You should be happy that one of our guests has found true love.
But I thought he was going to sweep ME off my feet, and I'd never have to work again!

Tut! Tut! That's just the stuff of dreams! You wouldn't REALLY have wanted to leave your home at Happyholme, now would you?
Wouldn't I?

Ah, here's my list! Vacuuming, dusting, cleaning windows, setting tables . . .
Oh — I guess not. I've worked like a slave for so long that I don't think I'd know what to do with myself if I didn't have all these jobs. Happy New Year, everyone!
THE END

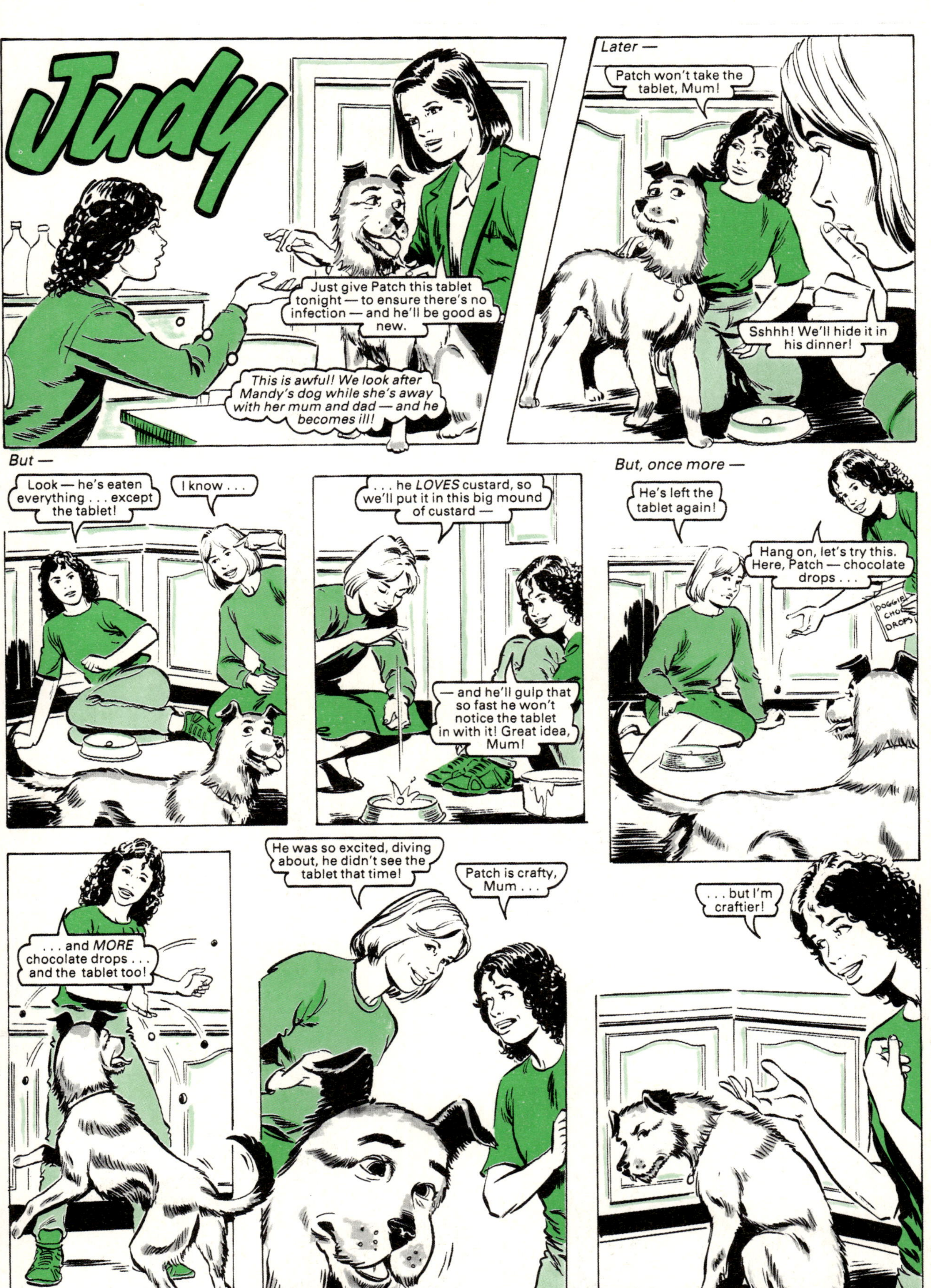
Judy
Just give Patch this tablet tonight — to ensure there's no infection — and he'll be good as new.
This is awful! We look after Mandy's dog while she's away with her mum and dad — and he becomes ill!
Later —
Patch won't take the tablet, Mum!
Sshhh! We'll hide it in his dinner!
But —
Look — he's eaten everything . . . except the tablet!
I know . . .
. . . he LOVES custard, so we'll put it in this big mound of custard —
— and he'll gulp that so fast he won't notice the tablet in with it! Great idea, Mum!
But, once more —
He's left the tablet again!
Hang on, let's try this. Here, Patch — chocolate drops . . .
DOGGIE CHOC DROPS
. . . and MORE chocolate drops . . . and the tablet too!
He was so excited, diving about, he didn't see the tablet that time!
Patch is crafty, Mum . . .
. . . but I'm craftier!

MY SECRET BOYFRIEND

A few days later —
Let's go shopping on Saturday. We can go into the **newsagent's, and** ogle Don.
Okay!
Want to come, Hattie?
Er . . . no thanks.
There's no point! If Don does ask someone out, it certainly won't be me!
Ooh! There's a car boot sale at Glendean School on Saturday. I'll go along there instead. I might be able to pick up some old postcards for my collection.
CAR BOOT SALE AT GLENDEAN SCHOOL SAT
Hi, Hattie! Penny for them!
A penny? Here you are, Nigel.
Eh? I don't want your money. I meant, a penny for your thoughts. In other words, what's on your mind? You looked interested in something.
Oh! Sorry. Um . . . er . . . well it w. . . was nothing important, Nigel.
What a clot I am! It's always the same when boys speak to me!
Did you see THAT?
Nigel Lewis is one of the easiest boys to talk to — but Hattie didn't manage to string two words together!
Saturday came, and at the car boot sale —
Excuse me — is that group of locomotive cards a complete set?
Yes, That's why the price is so high.
But it's NOT a complete set! There are two missing. It's daylight robbery at that price. I ought to warn that boy.

Don't buy them. It's *NOT* a complete set. I have a book about postcards. It lists all of the cards in lots of old sets. It's really useful.
I'll bet! I'd love to see it. I don't know the dates of half my collection. A book might help me catalogue them.

I don't live far from here. If you'd like to come with me, I'll show you my book.
Great!

Hey! What about the cards?
Sorry. Some other time perhaps.

Soon —
This book's fantastic! It's really great of you to let me look at it, Hattie.
My pleasure, Gary.
It is, too! For the first time in my life, I'm chatting to a boy without getting tongue-tied or acting silly. It must be because we share the same interest.

And, later, when it was time for Gary to go —
Will you come out with me? How about Monday evening?
That'd be ace! Thanks!
My first ever date! FANTASTIC!

On Monday —
What a let down Saturday was. We spent two hours hanging around in the newsagent's, and Don never even spoke to us.
You should have come to the car boot sale with me. *I* landed a date!

WHAT?
YOU?
He's a dream! I'm seeing him tonight. I'll tell you all about it tomorrow.
Their faces are a picture! For once, THEY are envious of ME!

That evening —
Enjoying your pizza?
Yes. It's great!
I wish those girls would stop staring over here though. What ARE they looking at?

Hattie soon found out —
Can we have your autograph?
We think your character's really great!
Oh! Er . . . yes, okay.

'Bye, girls! Come on, Hattie. Let's get out of here.
What's going on? I don't understand, Gary.

I'll explain. I've just started appearing in a TV soap.
What? I don't watch much TV — I'm too busy working on my postcard collection. I'd NO idea you were famous!

I know. It was obvious. That's why I fell for you. It was great to meet someone who shared the same interest as me — not who just liked me because I'm a TV star.
I'd like us to carry on going out, but can you keep it a secret from your friends? I don't want hordes of people turning up wherever we go.
Of course!
So, the next day —
How was your date?
When are you seeing him again, Hattie?
I . . . er . . . didn't have a date at all. I made it all up.
We should have guessed. No-one dishy would ever be interested in *HER*.
Let's go to the newsagent's. We can see Don *AND* buy a TV magazine. There's a feature on that new soap star Gary Gordon in it this week. He's ace!
After school —
I don't suppose Hattie wants to come. She'd rather rush home to her boring postcard collection.
I AM working on my collection tonight. But if only they knew who with!
THE END

JUDY
Going shopping, Judy? Can I come with you?
Sure, Mandy!

I want a belt. Ah! This one will do nicely.
Eh? It's a bit big and heavy for you.

It's not for me. It's for Jack! I want a shirt, too . . .
Who's Jack? What about Malcolm, Judy's boyfriend?
SALE
STON
WASH

Next stop — the record shop. There's a record Jack likes to dance to.
JACK?
That's all my shopping done! But I want to stop at the hairdresser's. I've decided to change my style. I can't look a mess for Jack!

Jack must be pretty special! You're buying him presents and you're changing your image for him. When do I get to meet him? Er — and what about Malcolm?
Come to the village hall on Saturday and see him there.

On Saturday—

It ISN'T disco night, after all, Tommy! The local drama group are performing their panto.
PANTOMIME
JACK
AND THE
BEANSTALK

NOW I get it! Judy hasn't fallen for Jack. She IS Jack! She's playing principal boy in the pantomime "Jack and the Beanstalk"! Ha! Ha!

BEST FRIENDS -

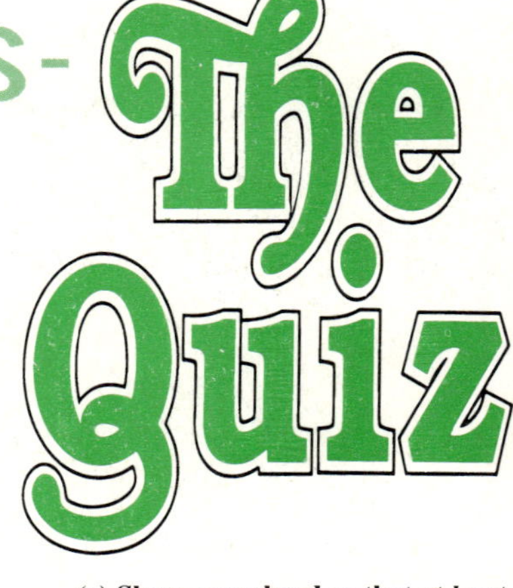

Do YOU make the perfect best friend? Try our light-hearted quiz to find out!

1. You and your best friend are going out for an evening. How do you decide where to go?
(a) You choose.
(b) You insist she chooses.
(c) You decide together.

2. Your best friend's broke, but you have ten pounds to spend. What do you do?
(a) Splash the whole lot on a pressie for her.
(b) Share the money with her.
(c) Spend it all on yourself — after all, it's YOUR money.

3. You start going steady with a boy you really fancy. Where does your best friend figure in all this?
(a) Nowhere!
(b) You insist she comes on all your dates.
(c) You don't see her as often as you did, but there are still several times a week when you DO get together.

4. Your friend tells you a secret and begs you not to repeat it. What do you do?
(a) Tell everyone.
(b) Try very hard not to tell anyone.
(c) Stick your mouth up with Sellotape so you can't POSSIBLY tell anyone.

5. Your best friend's heartbroken when she discovers she's got to wear glasses. What do you do?
(a) You tell her she'd look good in specs.
(b) You quote the old rhyme "Boys never make passes at girls who wear glasses."
(c) Even though you don't need specs, you get yourself a pair made of plain glass to keep her company.

6. Your best friend's dog dies suddenly. What's your course of action?
(a) You stuff your ears with cotton wool so you don't have to hear her blubbering on about it.
(b) You tell her she can share YOUR dog with you, if she likes.
(c) You sympathise, then — when the time is right — gently suggest a trip to the local dogs' home in the hope a new dog there will catch her eye.

7. Your best friend's ill. What do you do?
(a) You rush round with fifteen different kinds of medicine, seal the room to make it hygienic, and stay up all night with her.
(b) You go to visit her armed with magazines and fruit — but don't over-stay your welcome.
(c) You don't go near her. You don't want her germs!

8. Your friend's hopeless at maths, but it's your best subject. What do you do?
(a) Do all her maths homework for her.
(b) Tell her to work it out for herself.
(c) Offer help if she needs it.

9. Your best friend's had a new hair-do — but it's a disaster! What do you do?
(a) Suggest ways she could hide the worst of the damage with slides and ribbons.
(b) Remind her that hair only grows one centimetre a month, so she'll be stuck like this for ages.

(c) Shave your head so that at least you look worse than she does.

10. Your best friend borrows your favourite record and accidentally scratches it. What do you do?
(a) Accept it was an accident and forgive her.
(b) Scratch several more of your records so she'll know she's not the only one who does these things.
(c) Scratch several of HER records so she'll know she's not the only one who does these things!

11. Your best friend can't swim. What do you do?
(a) Push her in at the deep end.
(b) Offer to try teaching her.
(c) Buy her a rubber ring and three pairs of arm-bands for Christmas. She might not be able to swim — but at least she won't drown!

12. And finally — what about rows? Do you and your best friend ever have them?
(a) Never!
(b) Sometimes — but you soon make up afterwards.
(c) Only when she doesn't agree with your ideas.

How did you rate? Add up your score and check the total with the conclusions below!

Answers

1. (a) 1, (b) 3, (c) 2.
2. (a) 3, (b) 2, (c) 1.
3. (a) 1, (b) 3, (c) 2.
4. (a) 1, (b) 2, (c) 3.
5. (a) 2, (b) 1, (c) 3.
6. (a) 1, (b) 2, (c) 3.
7. (a) 3, (b) 2, (c) 1.
8. (a) 3, (b) 1, (c) 2.
9. (a) 2, (b) 1, (c) 3.
10. (a) 2, (b) 3, (c) 1.
11. (a) 1, (b) 2, (c) 3.
12. (a) 3, (b) 2, (c) 1.

Conclusions

29-36 You WANT to be a good best friend, but you tend to go a bit over the top! Cool it! All good friendships should have some give AND take. You deserve to be on the receiving end sometimes too. If you carry on as you are, you might end up killing your friendship by kindness.

20-28 Congratulations! You're the nicest best friend anyone could ever wish for!

12-19 Talk about an iceberg! Are you sure you even WANT to have a best friend? It seems to us the only person you like is yourself. Perhaps that's a good thing. Because — if you keep on like you are — you soon won't have any friends at all!

Surprise Party
SUSAN SMALL and her stepsister, Paula, were having a fancy dress party for their friends. But, on the day of the party, Susan didn't think she'd have the energy left to enjoy it!
Stepmother's off on one of her committees . . . the people from the catering agency who were supposed to arrange the party have let us down . . . and Paula's skived off somewhere, as usual!
So I'm left with the whole house to clean . . . the food to fix . . . the dishes and things to put out! It seems to be the story of my life!
A lot of hard work later—
I'll NEVER get it all done! And Mum said our guests are to leave their coats in Paula's room, so I'd better look in there too. That's usually a mess . . .
And—
Oh, it's worse than I expected! And look — "Judy"! So THIS is where my annual disappeared to! Typical of Paula to nick it!
JUDY

Susan couldn't resist reading the stories again—
right
"Judy" has always been my favourite. The characters are brill! Gosh, maybe I shouldn't have sat down, though . . .

All that housework . . . I'm so tired I can hardly keep my eyes open . . .

DING
DING
WHA . . . ?

It's the doorbell. How long have I been asleep? I'll have to work twice as hard now, to get things ready!

I'm coming!

Is this where the fancy dress party is?
Yes, but I'm sorry, you're too early.
FAR too early, the amount I've still got to do!

On the contrary, Susan, we're just in time! We should manage, though . . .

What a state this place is in! It would never do for *MY* young ladies!
I'll finish in there and you start the food, Nellie.

I've had plenty of practice with a duster in Happyholme . . .
Hang on . . .

You're Cindy Jones, aren't you? And the other girl's Nellie Perks . . . "Wee Slavey" in the "Judy"!

Er, let's just get the work done!
Cindy . . .
42

BEEP!
What is this contraption? Cook does not have anything of the sort!
A microwave. This is a modern kitchen. Maybe *YOU'D* better clean and *I'LL* cook.

Much later, when Paula returned—
Hey, the place looks good! And all this food, too! Did the agency people turn up after all?
No, Paula.

I'd better go and get dressed, then. The guests'll be here soon.
Watch those crumbs, will you?

You go and get *YOURSELF* dressed too, Susan.
I'm so grateful — to both of you.
A word of thanks. It isn't often *WE* hear that! But we wanted to help. We know what it's like, being left with everything to do!
The party was a huge success—
The food's brill!
Susan's done a triff job, hasn't she, Paula?
Er, yes. I helped, of course!

Everyone's enjoying themselves, Susan, but you look a bit sad.
Oh, I was just thinking I wish Simon was here. He was the only person I really wanted to invite, but Paula said *SHE* liked him too — and *SHE* wanted to invite him. So it seemed fairest that *NEITHER* of us did.

You mean, whoever gave him the invitation would have the best chance with him?
That's right, Cindy!

But, soon afterwards—
SIMON! What? I mean . . . what a nice surprise!
I was pleased to get Paula's invitation.

Paula's gone behind my back! I must have the most horrible stepsister in the world!
It could be worse, Susan . . . you could have TWO!

One is easier to handle. Listen . . .

So—
Oops! Sorry, Miss!
Oh, look! Who did that? I'll have to go and change.

Then—
Susan, will you dance? I wanted to ask you earlier, but Paula grabbed me . . .

After the party—
Do you want to come out with me tomorrow, Susan?
That would be lovely, Simon.

Next morning—
I feel so happy! The party last night was super. Everyone said so . . . including Simon! It all went so well I almost can't believe it was true . . .

One part of it CAN'T be true . . . Cindy and Nellie from "Judy" coming to life to help me! That's ridiculous!

Ooh — but there certainly WAS a party! Look at all this mess! And you know who'll get lumbered with cleaning it up . . . Muggins, of course!

DING
DING
There's the door now. I suppose I'll have to answer that as well!

Hi, Susan! Great party! We've come to help you clear up.
Lawks! You never thought we'd leave you to do it all yourself, surely, Miss Susan!
THE END

PEPPER THE PONY

BIG 'N' BERTHA
Dinner time, Big!
Huh! You spoil that mutt!
HEY! Watch it!
DOG

That hound has no manners!

Sheer greed! He's already had his meal.

Next day —
That hound doesn't eat until WE have had our meal. Nobody touch this dish.
DOG
But it's his dinner time, Dad!

Later —
Dinner's ready!
Great! I'm starving!

Dad! Wait a minute . . .
Lovely grub!

I tried to warn you. That's BIG'S dinner. You said to leave it where you put it!
UGH!
DOG

He'll just have to have YOUR dinner! That's what you get for being greedy!

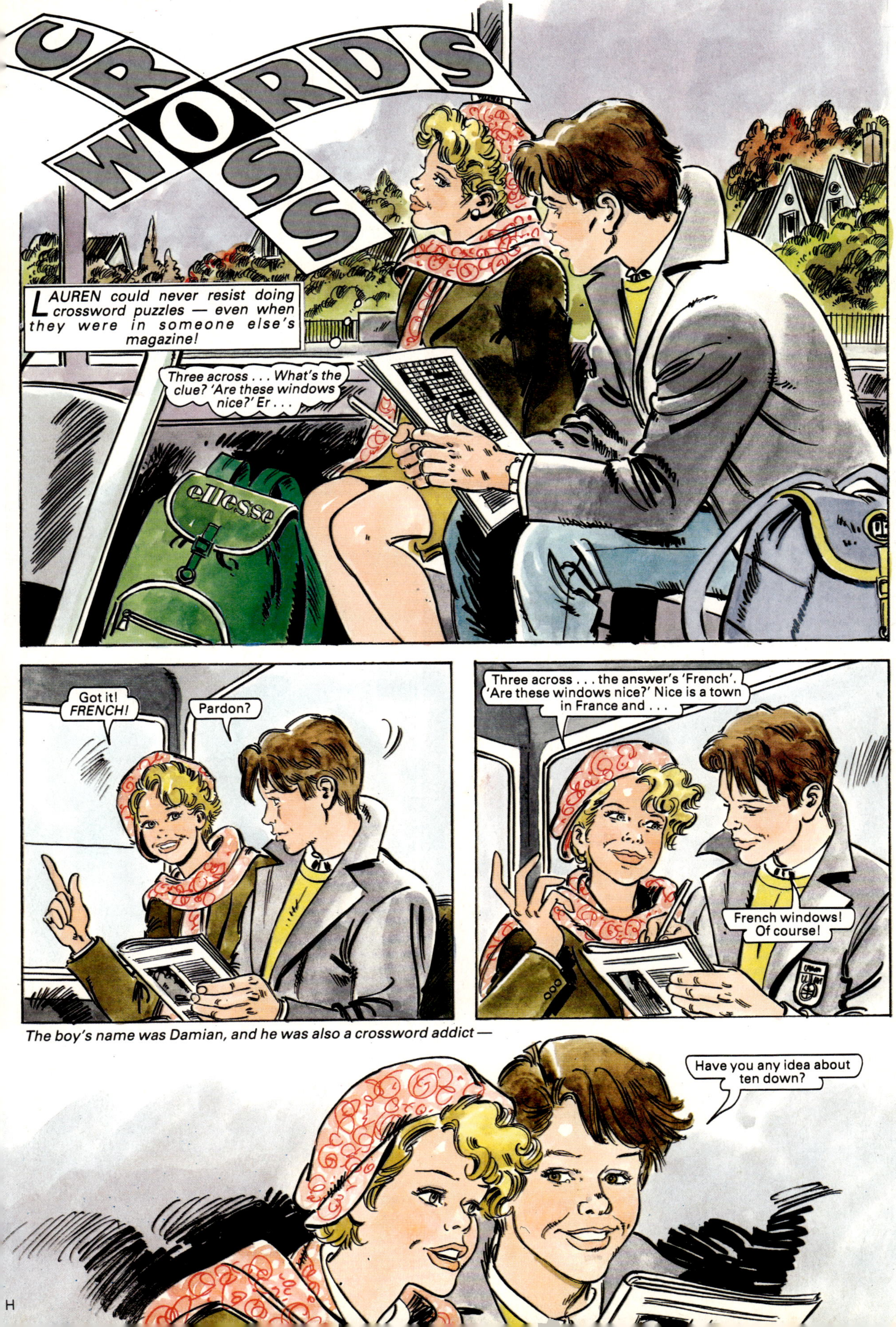

CROSS WORDS

LAUREN could never resist doing crossword puzzles — even when they were in someone else's magazine!

Three across . . . What's the clue? 'Are these windows nice?' Er . . .

eLLesse

The boy's name was Damian, and he was also a crossword addict —

They left at the same stop —
This is my usual bus, now we've moved house. If you're on it tomorrow, I'm sure we'll finish that crossword between us.
I will be!
Never mind French windows — he's rather NICE himself!

Every morning that week, they shared a crossword on the bus, and on Friday —
There's a huge crossword in the paper my mum and dad have every Saturday, but I can never get it finished by myself . . .
Are you asking me out, Damian?

If you'll come, Lauren.
Yes, I will!

They began dating regularly —
This is brill!
You can't do crosswords all the time!

And —

It's lovely here — and not a crossword in sight!

Then, one lunchtime —
Look, Lauren, there's — oh, no!

OCCHIO'S
It's Damian, with another girl!
Maybe it's his sister or something.

I think 'or something'! He's an ONLY child! And they're smiling at each other as though THEY'RE the ONLY people in the world!

That evening —
Hi! I've just got ONE clue to solve in the big prize crossword. But I just can't understand it.

Maybe you can explain it.
Maybe YOU can explain something to ME, first!

I was in Pinocchio's Pizzeria — yes. But I didn't see you.
You wouldn't! You were too busy gazing into her eyes!

The girl's name is Gail and we were joint winners of a competition Pinocchio's ran last month. It was a crossword, actually — on the back of their menu cards . . .

The prize was a meal in the restaurant, and they arranged a photographer from the local paper — for publicity . . .

So we had to look happy together, you see . . .
You certainly did THAT! But if you think I believe the rest of your story, you're mad! I've never heard such guff!

Soon —
And I'm never going out with you again!
You'll never have the chance!

You're back early! Is Damian with you?
No, he isn't! Let's say we've had CROSS WORDS.

Two days later —
Ah! Damian WAS telling the truth!
PIZZA PARLOUR PRIZE WINNERS

I wish I'd listened! I really miss him . . .
PIZZA PARLOUR PRIZE WINNERS

But I'm NOT going to apologise to him first. He shouldn't have flown off the handle the way he did.

Meanwhile, at Damian's house —
PIZZA PARLOUR PRIZE WINNERS
I wish I'd never had the wretched free pizza — it made me feel sick anyway. And I really miss Lauren . . .

. . . but I'm not going creeping and apologising to her. After all, I didn't do anything WRONG.

So, on the bus next day —
Lauren's so nice, but . . .
I do still like Damian, but . . .
Can I squeeze in here?

Now, two down — 'An apology' . . . five letters . . . begins with the letter 'S' —

SORRY!
THE END

She's No Angel!

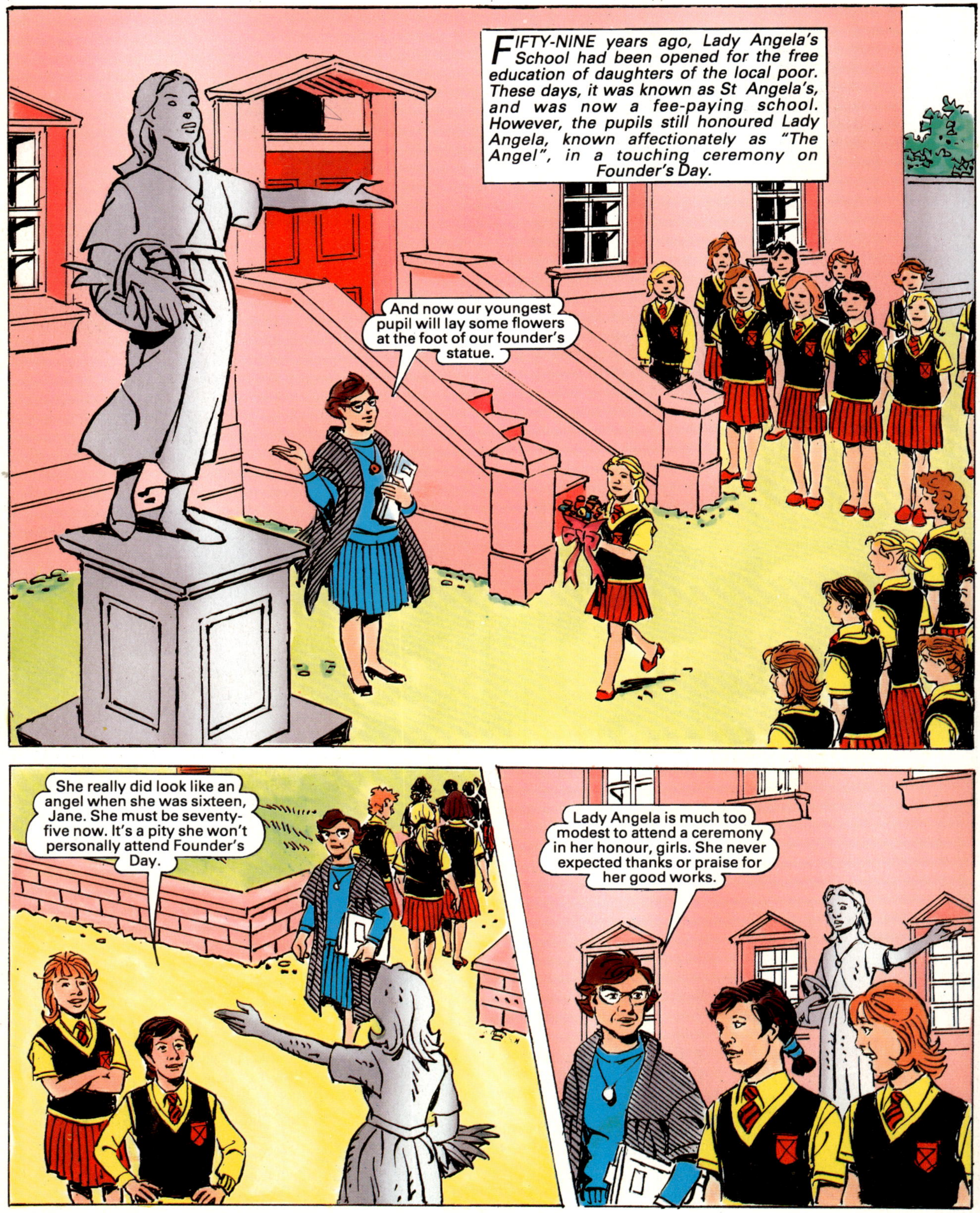

FIFTY-NINE years ago, Lady Angela's School had been opened for the free education of daughters of the local poor. These days, it was known as St Angela's, and was now a fee-paying school. However, the pupils still honoured Lady Angela, known affectionately as "The Angel", in a touching ceremony on Founder's Day.

And now our youngest pupil will lay some flowers at the foot of our founder's statue.

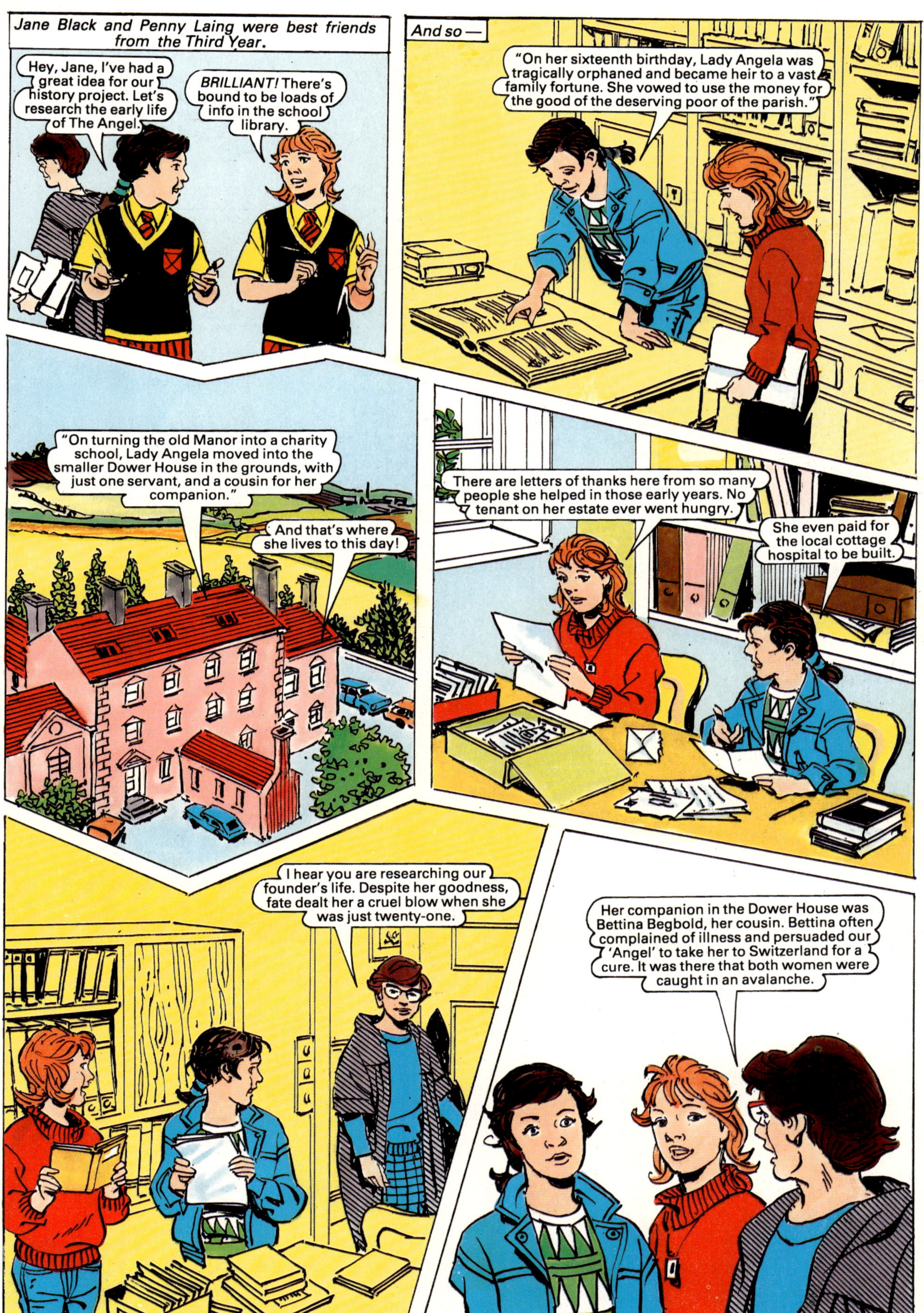
Jane Black and Penny Laing were best friends from the Third Year.
Hey, Jane, I've had a great idea for our history project. Let's research the early life of The Angel.
BRILLIANT! There's bound to be loads of info in the school library.
And so —
"On her sixteenth birthday, Lady Angela was tragically orphaned and became heir to a vast family fortune. She vowed to use the money for the good of the deserving poor of the parish."
"On turning the old Manor into a charity school, Lady Angela moved into the smaller Dower House in the grounds, with just one servant, and a cousin for her companion."
And that's where she lives to this day!
There are letters of thanks here from so many people she helped in those early years. No tenant on her estate ever went hungry.
She even paid for the local cottage hospital to be built.
I hear you are researching our founder's life. Despite her goodness, fate dealt her a cruel blow when she was just twenty-one.
Her companion in the Dower House was Bettina Begbold, her cousin. Bettina often complained of illness and persuaded our 'Angel' to take her to Switzerland for a cure. It was there that both women were caught in an avalanche.

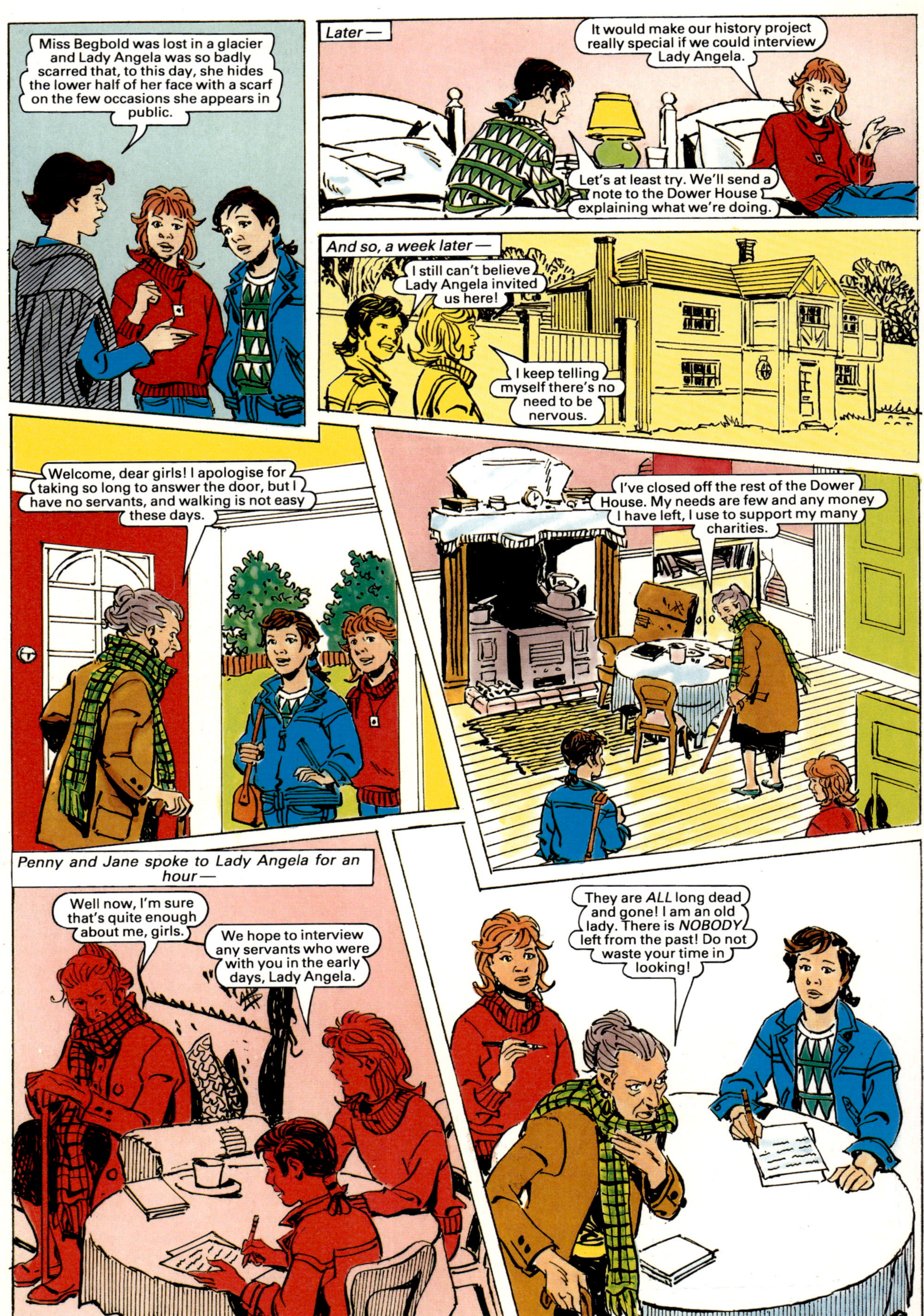
Miss Begbold was lost in a glacier and Lady Angela was so badly scarred that, to this day, she hides the lower half of her face with a scarf on the few occasions she appears in public.
Later —
It would make our history project really special if we could interview Lady Angela.
Let's at least try. We'll send a note to the Dower House explaining what we're doing.
And so, a week later —
I still can't believe Lady Angela invited us here!
I keep telling myself there's no need to be nervous.
Welcome, dear girls! I apologise for taking so long to answer the door, but I have no servants, and walking is not easy these days.
I've closed off the rest of the Dower House. My needs are few and any money I have left, I use to support my many charities.
Penny and Jane spoke to Lady Angela for an hour —
Well now, I'm sure that's quite enough about me, girls.
We hope to interview any servants who were with you in the early days, Lady Angela.
They are ALL long dead and gone! I am an old lady. There is NOBODY left from the past! Do not waste your time in looking!

And now before you leave, I insist on fetching a little refreshment. A glass of milk, perhaps?
Oh — er, thank you.

Imagine being an heiress and choosing to end up like this because you've given all your money to charity. Lady Angela truly is an angel!
I think there's a cat shut behind these doors. I'll let it out. Coming, Puss!

When Jane opened the doors, the girls stared in amazement —
It's fantastic! These all look like valuable antiques!

Through here there's a modern luxury kitchen. It's a self-contained apartment belonging to someone with loads of money!

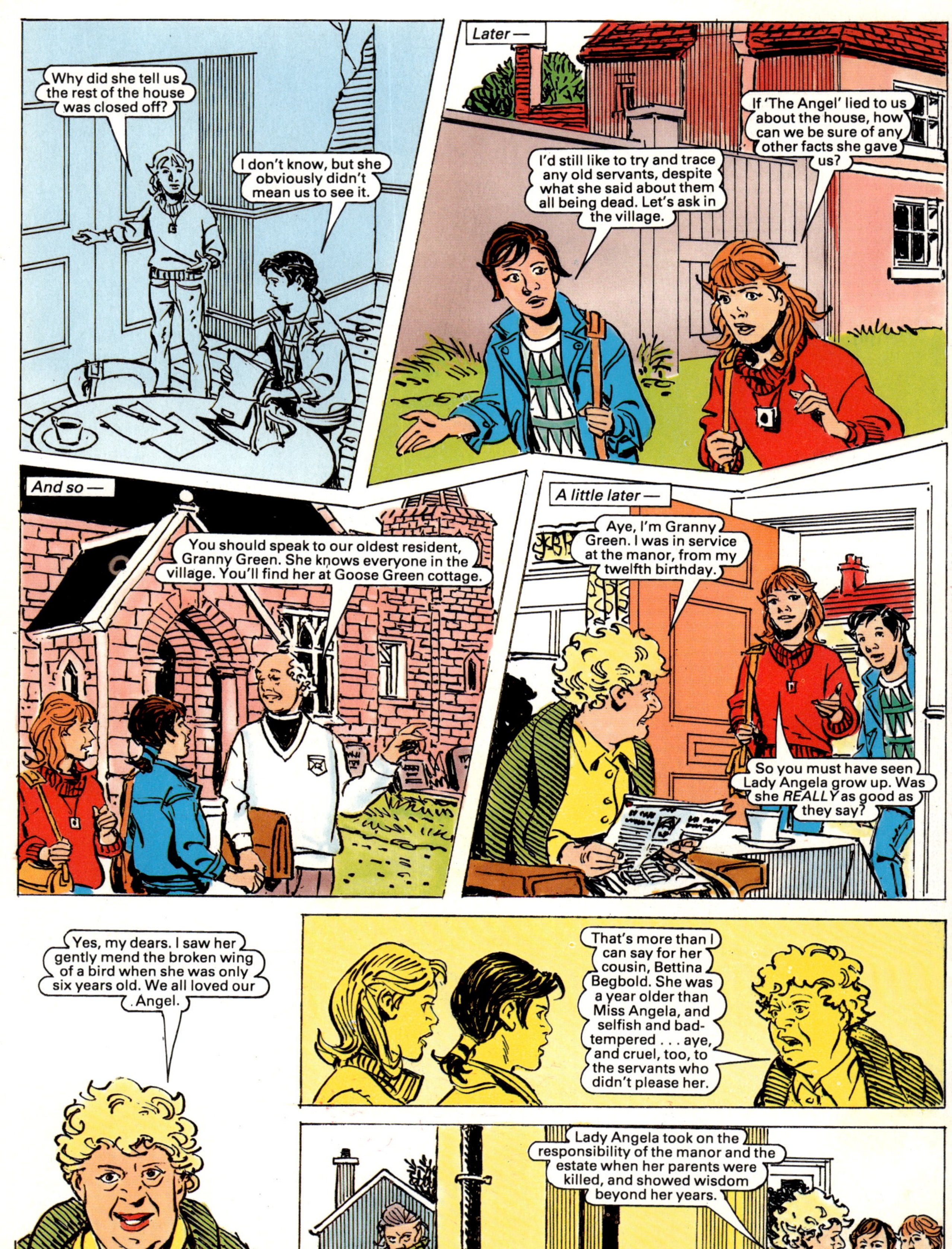
Why did she tell us the rest of the house was closed off?
I don't know, but she obviously didn't mean us to see it.
Later —
I'd still like to try and trace any old servants, despite what she said about them all being dead. Let's ask in the village.
If 'The Angel' lied to us about the house, how can we be sure of any other facts she gave us?
And so —
You should speak to our oldest resident, Granny Green. She knows everyone in the village. You'll find her at Goose Green cottage.
A little later —
Aye, I'm Granny Green. I was in service at the manor, from my twelfth birthday.
So you must have seen Lady Angela grow up. Was she *REALLY* as good as they say?
Yes, my dears. I saw her gently mend the broken wing of a bird when she was only six years old. We all loved our Angel.
That's more than I can say for her cousin, Bettina Begbold. She was a year older than Miss Angela, and selfish and bad-tempered . . . aye, and cruel, too, to the servants who didn't please her.
Lady Angela took on the responsibility of the manor and the estate when her parents were killed, and showed wisdom beyond her years.

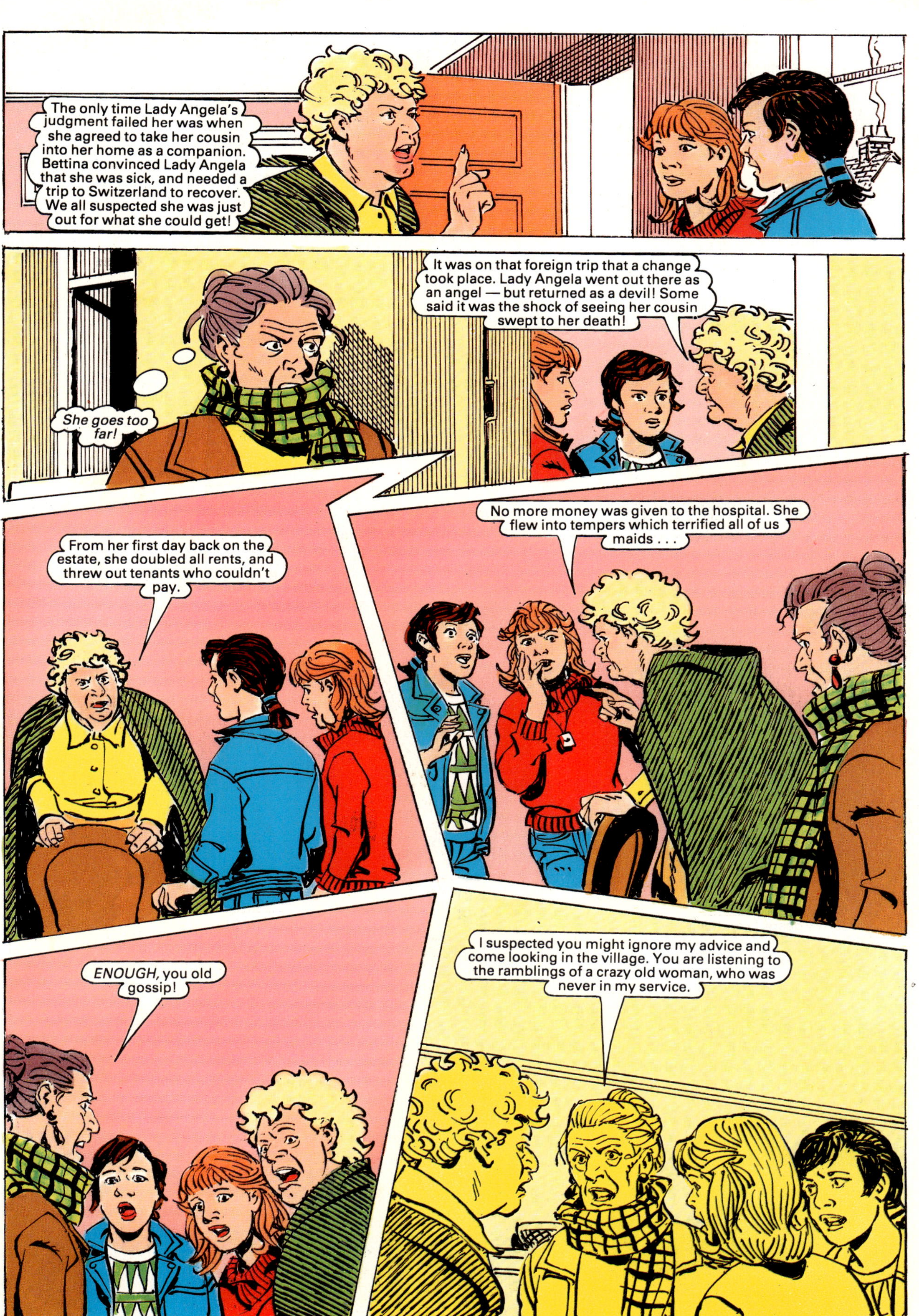
The only time Lady Angela's judgment failed her was when she agreed to take her cousin into her home as a companion. Bettina convinced Lady Angela that she was sick, and needed a trip to Switzerland to recover. We all suspected she was just out for what she could get!
It was on that foreign trip that a change took place. Lady Angela went out there as an angel — but returned as a devil! Some said it was the shock of seeing her cousin swept to her death!
She goes too far!
From her first day back on the estate, she doubled all rents, and threw out tenants who couldn't pay.
No more money was given to the hospital. She flew into tempers which terrified all of us maids . . .
ENOUGH, you old gossip!
I suspected you might ignore my advice and come looking in the village. You are listening to the ramblings of a crazy old woman, who was never in my service.

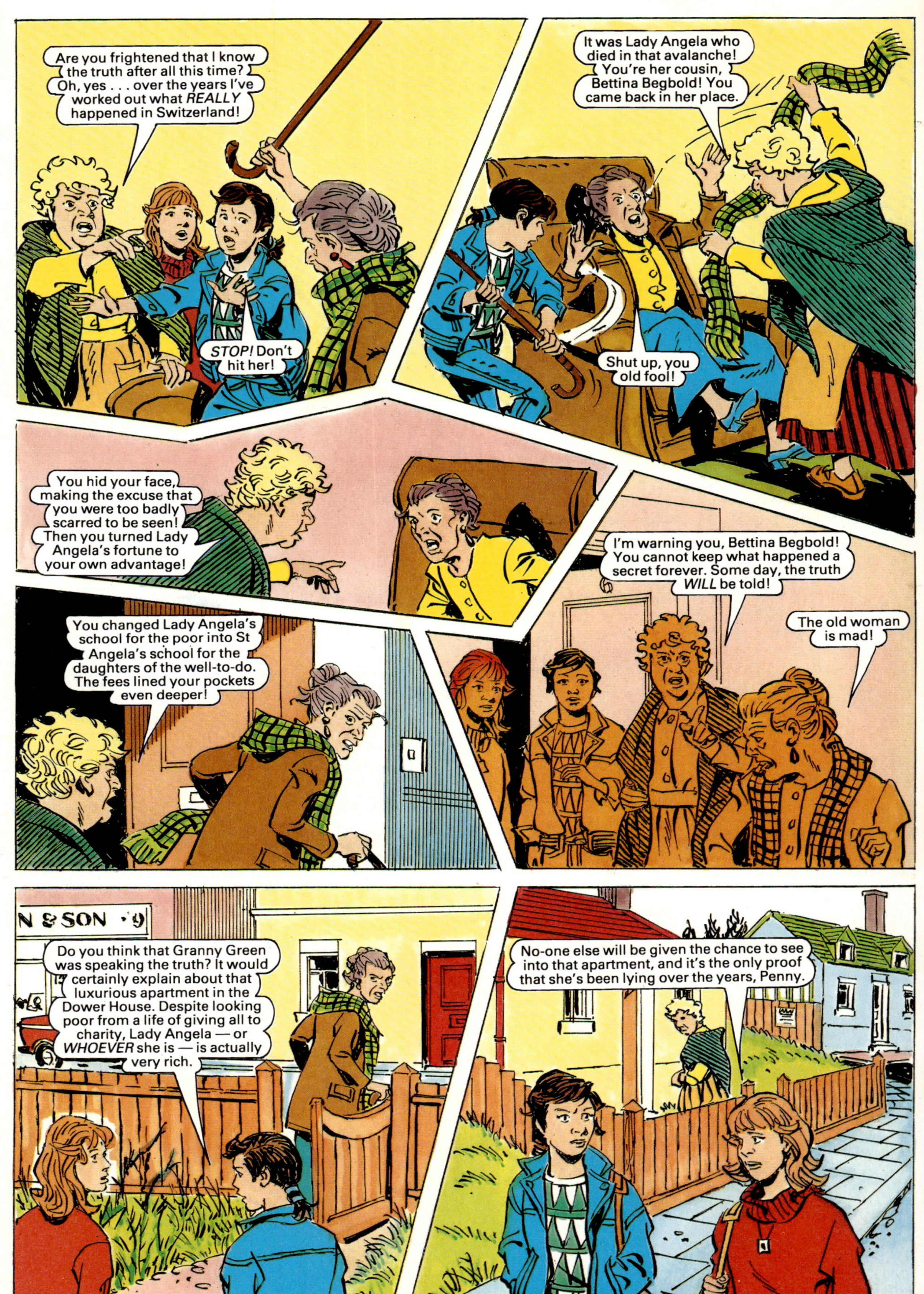
Are you frightened that I know the truth after all this time? Oh, yes . . . over the years I've worked out what *REALLY* happened in Switzerland!
STOP! Don't hit her!
It was Lady Angela who died in that avalanche! You're her cousin, Bettina Begbold! You came back in her place.
Shut up, you old fool!
You hid your face, making the excuse that you were too badly scarred to be seen! Then you turned Lady Angela's fortune to your own advantage!
I'm warning you, Bettina Begbold! You cannot keep what happened a secret forever. Some day, the truth *WILL* be told!
You changed Lady Angela's school for the poor into St Angela's school for the daughters of the well-to-do. The fees lined your pockets even deeper!
The old woman is mad!
N & SON '9
Do you think that Granny Green was speaking the truth? It would certainly explain about that luxurious apartment in the Dower House. Despite looking poor from a life of giving all to charity, Lady Angela — or *WHOEVER* she is — is actually very rich.
No-one else will be given the chance to see into that apartment, and it's the only proof that she's been lying over the years, Penny.

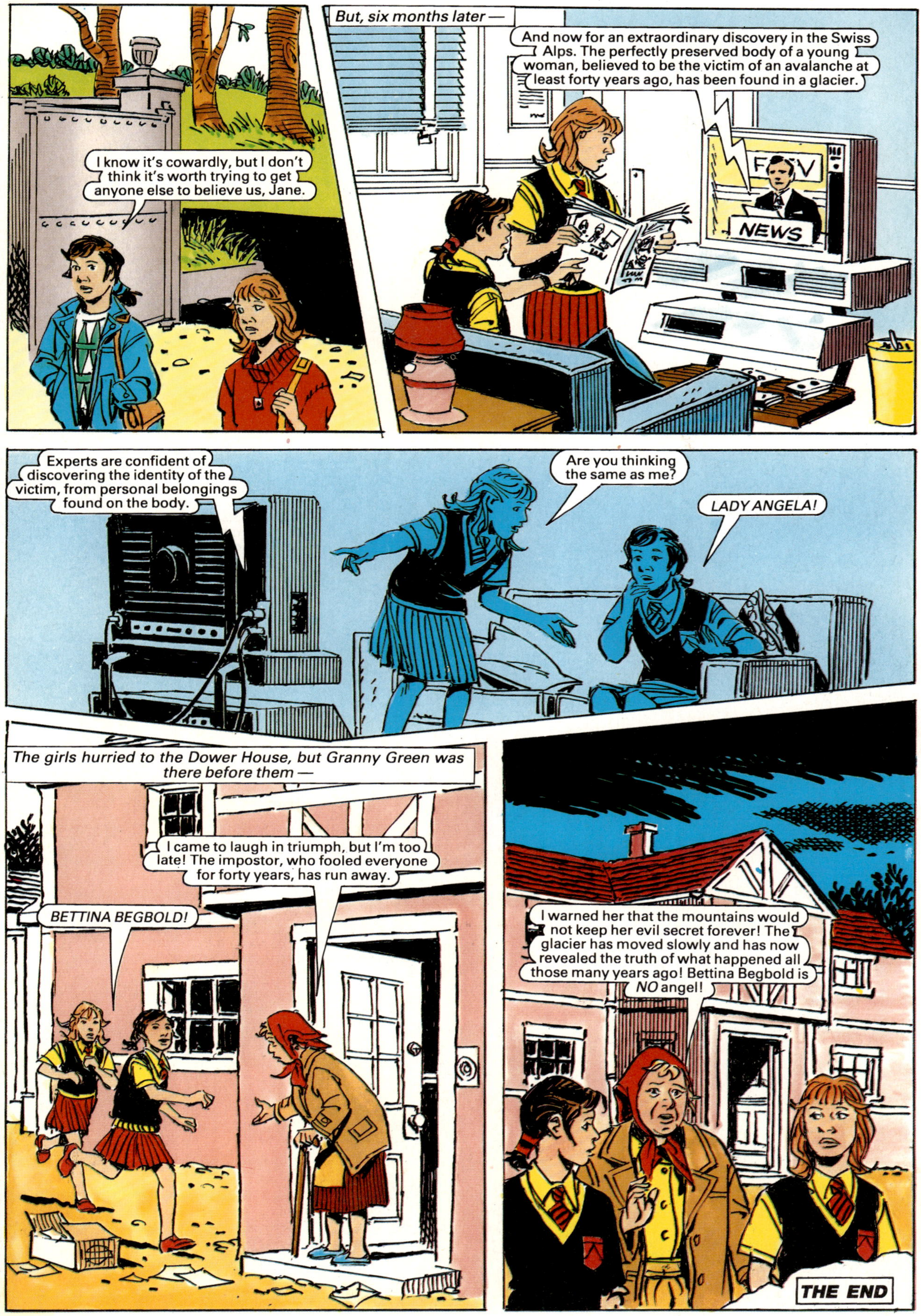

Experts are confident of discovering the identity of the victim, from personal belongings found on the body.

Are you thinking the same as me?

LADY ANGELA!

The girls hurried to the Dower House, but Granny Green was there before them —

I came to laugh in triumph, but I'm too late! The impostor, who fooled everyone for forty years, has run away.

BETTINA BEGBOLD!

I warned her that the mountains would not keep her evil secret forever! The glacier has moved slowly and has now revealed the truth of what happened all those many years ago! Bettina Begbold is *NO* angel!

THE END

JUDY
JUDY
A DOG IS FOR LIFE...
JUDY
JUDY FOR GIRLS 1993
JUDY
JUDY
JUDY FOR GIRLS 1993